"There are things within us all that can never be unleashed."

-Vanessa Ives

THE

FEMININE

MACABRE

A WOMAN'S JOURNAL OF ALL THINGS
STRANGE AND UNUSUAL

CURATED BY
AMANDA R. WOOMER

WITH FOREWORD BY
LISA MORTON

VOLUME IV

To the undesirables lost to history.

OTHER BOOKS FROM SPOOK-EATS

CONTENTS

FOREWORD

A few years ago, I found myself in the curious (and slightly panic-stricken) situation of researching two books, both with rapidly approaching deadlines, at the same time. One book, *Calling the Spirits: A History of Séances*, was a non-fiction historical overview; the other, *Weird Women: Classic Supernatural Fiction from Groundbreaking Female Writers 1852-1923,* was an anthology of short stories I was co-editing with my friend Les Klinger. At first glance, these two books might seem to have nothing more in common than ghosts, but as I made my way through working on both, I found something unexpected and surprising that they shared: both were (in part) about women who had escaped the strangling strictures of the 19th Century and made some incredible contributions that would be later overshadowed by those of their male peers.

We're all aware of the tight hold that Victorian society exercised on women, who were typically confined to the roles of daughter, wife, domestic, or factory worker, but some found ingenious ways to live outside those prescribed boundaries. Take, for example, Florence Cook, one of my favorite 19th Century mediums: Florence was a young, pretty, and charismatic teenager from a middle-class London family who found fame as a medium. Florence, who was probably born in 1856, was likely destined for marriage and motherhood, but instead, she used her abilities as a medium (or an actress, if you're on the skeptical side) to become a genuine celebrity in Spiritualist circles. She called the spirits for lords and ladies, for writers and scientists; she acquired a patron who paid her thousands of pounds in exchange for messages from the beyond. In 1874, the esteemed physicist and chemist William Crookes (later to be knighted) investigated Florence thoroughly, even photographing himself arm in arm with her spirit guide Katie King (who happened to bear a remarkable resemblance to Florence); Crookes ended up pronouncing Florence completely genuine, endangering his own reputation in the process (witnesses later claimed that Florence confessed to having an affair with Crookes during the testing in Crookes's home).

Compare that to the story of Emma Frances Dawson, an American author who moved from Maine to California in the 1870s with her divorced mother and took up writing short stories for magazines as a way to support them both (yes, it was possible back then to make a living as a writer of short stories!). Dawson never wrote a novel but produced a number of supernatural short stories that were greatly admired by her peers (who included the famed author Ambrose Bierce). Although Dawson's 1897 collection *An Itinerant House and Other Stories* is now highly prized by collectors, very few scholars of supernatural fiction know her astonishing work. Meanwhile, Bierce's name is recognizable to even casual fans of horror fiction.

What these concurrent women's stories made me think about was how often those of us who have pursued the paranormal, as either purveyors of real-life experiences or fictitious ones, have been pushed aside by history. For every Sylvia Browne or Shirley Jackson (whose 1959 classic novel *The Haunting of Hill House* remains the finest work of fiction ever written about a paranormal investigation), there are dozens if not hundreds of Georgiana Houghtons, Helen Duncans, Eleanor Sidgwicks, and Catherine Crowes on the real side, and Dinah Mulocks (who wrote what Charles Dickens called "the best ghost story ever written"), Rhoda Broughtons, Mary Elizabeth Braddons, and Florence Marryats on the literary side. Why are these women less commemorated now than the men who also investigated and wrote alongside them?

I'm so pleased to say that I believe the tides are turning at last. There are more and more studies of the contributions that women have made to these areas (if you'd like to know more about the history of great women horror writers, I highly recommend Lisa Kröger and Melanie R. Anderson's *Monster She Wrote*). One of the things I love about *The Feminine Macabre* journals is that they form a cross-over between my two interests: celebrating the history of women in the paranormal with excellent writing from contemporary woman-identifying authors. In the past, there was often considerable overlap between Spiritualists and writers—Marie Corelli, one of the bestselling authors of the 1890s, was an ardent Spiritualist, and Florence Marryat, mentioned above, was a great admirer of Florence Cook. Now, more than a century after these remarkable women were shaping how we think about the supernatural, we are their spiritual descendants.

Here's hoping *The Feminine Macabre* continues through dozens of volumes because there's still a whole lot of neglect and misconceptions to set right.

Lisa Morton

INTRODUCTION

As I sit in my office with a cloud of incense smoke wafting around my head, surrounded by my spooky library, Victorian hair art, and horror movie memorabilia on the walls, I can't help but think of the importance behind the number four.

Some say it's an "Angel Number," while others just roll their eyes at the concept. But there's no denying that four has always been a significant number throughout history in the occult, religions, and even nature.

In numerology, four represents strength and stability; it is deeply rooted and (ironically) tied to masculine energy. In astrology, the number four is connected to the North Node, pointing you toward your lifelong journey. The Ancient Egyptians believed that Heaven was supported by four pillars rising from the earth. In Tarot, the number four symbolizes hard work, high expectations, and (once again) stability. We have four seasons and four cardinal points. Four-leaf clovers. Four Horsemen of the Apocalypse. Four Noble Truths. Canopic jars were used in groups of four. To the Pueblo people, the number four was sacred. The London Fire lasted four days. Four US Presidents have been assassinated (sidenote: I'm the great-niece of one of those assassins). There were said to be four rivers that flowed from the Garden of Eden. Freyja spent four nights with the dwarves, making love, before walking away with the necklace Brisingamen. Even the Pythagoreans believed the number four was perfect and that it symbolized God.

Now I'm not saying that our fourth volume of *The Feminine Macabre* is perfect or god-like (though it is yet another fascinating volume if you ask me). But maybe there is something to it.

We're four volumes in now—a fourth attempt to create a journal we can be proud of and one that we hope you'll enjoy. Like the four in numerology, we're relatively stable now, and while it's taken a lot of hard work and dedication (as symbolized in Tarot), I think we can keep this going for a while. As a journal, we're growing internationally (as seen in the four cardinal points)—not only do we have writers from the United States, Canada, the United Kingdom, France, and Ireland, but we've also branched out to Belgium and Australia. And while your North Node (connected to the number four in astrology) might not say that your lifelong journey has led you to read (or write for0 *The Feminine Macabre*, it might be a starting point for blossoming writers that <u>will</u> go on to have a writing career. And perhaps the success of this journal is thanks to a bit of luck (four-leaf clovers), I'd say more than anything, it's the strength and deeply-rooted beliefs (numerology) that these writers and researchers have that has made *The Feminine Macabre* what it is.

If this is your first time entering the world of *The Feminine Macabre*: Welcome! We're so happy you could join us along with Lisa Morton and 35 other female and nonbinary researchers in the field (our youngest contributor being only 14 years old!). And if you've been with us since the beginning, thank you. Who knows? Maybe four is our lucky number!

Amanda R Woomer

Spook-Eats
September 2022

An Important Note

Some of the subject matter and images herein may be disturbing to some readers. Discretion is advised.

The views expressed by the writers in this journal do not necessarily reflect the views held by Spook-Eats. The paranormal is a field of constant growth with ever-changing theories and ideas. The opinions expressed within these pages belong to the authors who pen them. We encourage you to come to your own conclusions.

THE

FEMININE

MACABRE

A WOMAN'S JOURNAL OF ALL THINGS
STRANGE AND UNUSUAL

CURATED BY
AMANDA R. WOOMER

WITH FOREWORD BY
LISA MORTON

VOLUME IV

An Unnamed Sorrow Where Marian Adams Should Be

Leanna Renee Hieber

In a verdant corner of Rock Creek Cemetery in Washington, D.C., a curious sculpture sits upright against its own stone wall, bordered by evergreen holly trees and creeping ivy. The androgynous figure in bronze, hooded and shrouded as if sitting on a rocky dais in its own winding-sheets, is notably eerie and untitled. Some call the figure "grief," others associate the form with "sorrow" and feel the heavy weight of the figure's presence. Sculpted by one of the 19th Century's most celebrated sculptors, Augustus Saint-Gaudens, the sculpture was erected as the sole monument to a very real woman of intelligence and station who passed away under mysterious circumstances in 1885—Marian Hooper Adams.

Photo courtesy of Library of Congress, Prints & Photographs Division, DC, WASH, 384-4

But she isn't named anywhere on her own monument.

Marian was a celebrated socialite, a talented photographer at the forefront of the medium, very familiar with the chemicals and processes of developing her own images. She is thought to be the inspiration for Henry James' *Daisy Miller* and possibly *The Portrait of a Lady*. Her marriage to writer, historian, and academic Henry Adams, from all accounts and letters shared with friends and family, was a happy one. Their home in Washington was filled with intellectuals and interesting people.

Henry traveled a great deal, and at some point, Marian's health— perhaps mental as well as physical—took a turn, particularly after the death of Marian's father, with whom she was very close. A certain gulf grew that could not be crossed.

While it was reported in the paper at the time that Marian was found dead, having suffered from "paralysis of the heart," it was later determined that she had taken her own life. While ill, alone in her bedroom, she swallowed lethal chemicals that were a part of her photography development process and was found by her husband, her body prone before the fireplace.

As is often the case with notable socially well-connected people, gossip was rife, and ghost stories were prevalent. The

Marian Hooper Adams (1843-1885) on horseback at Beverly Farms. Tintype by unidentified photographer, October 1869.

Adams' house was soon deemed haunted, dark most of the time as Henry continued to travel. He paid no mind to the gossip surrounding his wife's death or the disembodied sounds of sobs said to have been mysteriously emanating from the house after the tragedy.

The cemetery itself at first fought Adams when he presented his wife's curious memorial, but his insistence won out. The figure sits in mystery with no name, no title, no dates of birth or death, just sitting as if waiting to be called forth to some inscrutable purpose.

Adams did nothing to dissuade anyone's belief in his eccentricity—a kinder word than self-absorption—as the man made no reference to his wife whatsoever in his autobiography. It was as if she'd never existed. The most charitable thing one could say is that it was perhaps too painful for him to speak about her or her passing—historical documents do attest to the fact that he loved her. But the choice not to name her erases her from history, and that is a selfish act. She was praised as an insightful and discerning intellect and a magnificent photographer who, while her husband discouraged her from publishing her photographs, still captured important figures of the day and chronicled women's places in a changing world.

Gaudens' sculpture is famous and evocative, but the shrouded figure's mysterious and brooding presence, coupled with the lack of attribution to the woman who it supposedly honors, draws a focus away from Marian and becomes something else entirely.

> ### THE VOID WHERE MARIAN'S NAME SHOULD BE IS FILLED WITH A RESTLESS UNEASE.

Those who visit the graveyard describe a heavy weight often felt before the statue, admittedly lovely in a forlorn and gothic way, is even in view. An unsettled nature is often attributed to the statue, most visitors not knowing any of the history around it, just finding themselves troubled by the sight of the shrouded form and not really knowing why.

When my co-author Andrea Janes and I sat down to write *A Haunted History of Invisible Women: True Stories of America's Ghosts*, which offers a selection of women's ghost stories around the United States, I wanted Marian to be included, but we couldn't work her story into the sections we'd already agreed upon. So, I feel I owe her this text because so much of our book is about naming the underserved or forgotten, clarifying misinformation about women's history, and bringing forth as much truth as we can gather about who these women *were* before talking about the ghosts they *are*. I don't know that I can categorize Marian's ghost, per se, nor can anyone conclusively confirm that she haunts the cemetery, but *I* am certainly unsettled that she's not named on her own memorial. It feels like unfinished business, a trope that sits at the heart of countless ghost stories. Stories of sensing or picturing a sad presence while sitting by the sculpture permeate D.C. ghostlore.

Ghosts often want to be acknowledged. That's something I keep returning to when discussing the paranormal. Spirits wish to be noticed. Addressed. All the more so if their name and history have been effectively erased—a mysterious sculpture standing in for anything they may have wanted the world to know about them. Perhaps in this transposition of personhood to vague artistic reference, the idea of Marian is made infamous, but she herself is not *known*.

I find it worth noting that it's holly trees that surround the statue, and ivy is also prevalent in the surrounding environs. Holly is a particularly protective plant in magical thinking, and while Marian is not named anywhere on that slab, perhaps whatever energy remains around that statue and its dais is held in protective aggregate by the surrounding plants. Holly and ivy—not just the stuff of a Christmas carol, but two plants with deep meanings of protection, fidelity, and evergreen, eternal life. Marian's mother was a transcendentalist poet who died

Self-portrait of Marian "Clover" Adams, c. 1860.
Photo courtesy of the Massachusetts Historical Society

when Marian was young, and perhaps that legacy would find comfort in the natural world that is watching over that curious grave marker.

At the heart of any good ghost story, I've found in my work as an author, lecturer, and ghost tour guide around the country, are the questions asked about the unknown with no promise of an answer. The untitled sculpture at an unnamed grave is, in and of itself, an unanswered question. It is an active query, which gives it a certain life-force. It is animate in that it remains such a *curious* choice for a loved one to leave behind. To this day, no one really knows what to think about it.

In a 1908 letter Adams wrote to Saint-Gaudens' son Homer, Henry demanded: "Do not allow the world to tag my figure with a name! Every magazine writer wants to label it as some American patent medicine for popular consumption… Your father meant it to ask a question, not to give an answer; and the man who answers will be damned to eternity like the men who answered the Sphinx."

It is noted in this letter as *his* figure, and he only mentions men asking questions about his wife's monument. She remains absent from the conversation, even in the hypothetical and philosophical.

When you visit D.C., please give the statue a visit and say Marian's name. It won't etch any letters into the stone, but perhaps we can build on collective memory and allow for a woman not to just be a sidenote or an unanswered question but her own person again.

DEATH DISPLAYED: HUMAN REMAINS ASSOCIATED WITH WITCHCRAFT EXHIBITED AT MUSEUMS

Aoife Sutton

When we think of human remains on display in museums, an image of a skeleton or mummy from an era far back in time often comes to mind. Archaeological remains thousands of years old are often at the forefront of the conversation. Still, there are collections of human remains from more recent times that were used in the practice of witchcraft or associated with the practice.

Often, charms could be made from human hair, which is non-destructive in retrieval, but retained specimens could also be something more destructive and painful to obtain, such as bone or skin. Even reconstructed human remains can be very unsettling, as is often the case in wax anatomical and pathological specimens in medical museums—this is something I have observed during my research trips.

In this brief essay, I will look at five examples of human remains artifacts (or depicted human remains) in museums associated with witchcraft. The museums I have selected are:

The Museum of Witchcraft and Magic (Cornwall, UK)

The Museum of Icelandic Sorcery and Witchcraft (Iceland)

The Pitt Rivers Museum (Oxford, UK)

The Museum of London (London, UK)

Red Hair Charm
Museum of Witchcraft and Magic, Cornwall

The first item is a lock of red hair in a small, white bag—the museum refers to it as a "charm." It is recorded as belonging to a virgin, and, coupled with the fact the woman was a redhead, it was thought to be very powerful. The charm was meant for a male virgin so he could have a long and happy marriage with many opportunities in life.

The Museum of Witchcraft and Magic is located in Cornwall, UK. The museum website states the center aims "to represent the diversity and vigor of magical practice respectfully, accurately, and impartially."

> HAIR HAS OFTEN BEEN THOUGHT TO CONTAIN A MYSTIC LINK WITH THE BODY EVEN AFTER BEING CUT FROM THE LIVING OR THE DEAD.

Many loved ones retain hair cuttings upon a family member's death as a *memento mori*, and mothers often keep the locks of their baby's first haircut. Hair was often incorporated into image magic and used in a witches' bottle—for malevolent or protective means.

Fiery and temperamental personality traits have often been associated with redheads in history—with many red-haired women accused of witchcraft based solely upon the fact they were redheaded. Hair is a huge part of identity, with many victims of the witchcraft trials having had their hair cut off or their scalp shaved as part of emotional torture, viewing of "witch marks," or simply to prevent the spread of headlice in prison.

REPRODUCTION OF HUMAN SKIN PANTS OR "NECROPANTS"
THE MUSEUM OF ICELANDIC SORCERY AND WITCHCRAFT, ICELAND

Unlike other witch hunts across the world, the witch hunts in Iceland primarily targeted men in the 17th Century. At the Museum of Icelandic Sorcery and Witchcraft, there is a particularly harrowing reconstruction of "necropants"—although a reconstruction, the exhibit is particularly grotesque.

The reconstruction shows bare legs from the waist down with hair, scrotum, and penis realistically depicted. The pants are reconstructed as it was thought that the skinning of the lower half of a corpse was part of a ritual to attract wealth. The witch would place a coin in the scrotum along with a piece of parchment with a stave on it before putting the pants on skin to skin. The pants would continuously produce coins from the scrotum.

Although not made from real skin in this instance, the exhibit itself is shocking and illustrates what witches were thought to do in past societies. The act of wearing someone's skin in such a way is disturbing, and coupled with the shocking depiction of the body parts, it makes for quite unsettling viewing.

Modern Day Witch Bottle with Teeth
Museum of London, London

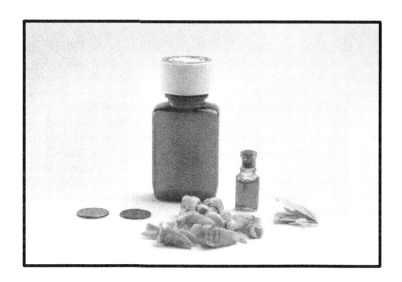

Witch bottles and their remains are often linked to the 17th Century and are not often thought of as being a modern plastic pill bottle like this example held at the Museum of London.

A large number of human teeth, coins, and clove oil were found in the bottle, which was deposited in the river Thames. It was found on the riverbank in the 1980s. The inclusion of clove oil with the teeth may suggest this bottle was created to assist with a toothache or gum disease.

The bottle and the contents were exhibited as part of *Spellbound: Magic, Ritual, and Witchcraft* which ran between August 2018 and January 2019 at the Ashmolean Museum in Oxford. The witch bottle from Margaret Murray's collection was also exhibited with *Spellbound* (see object 4).

Teeth are that unusual human tissue that can be removed painfully or fall out naturally—they have often been associated with protection in battle or used against a curse of some sort. Baby teeth are left under the pillow for a folkloric figure to come and retrieve, and babies whose teeth came through on the upper gums first were sometimes viewed with suspicion. Teeth leave a life signature on the human body and are often examined by archaeologists via isotopic analysis, tooth wear analysis, and through DNA extraction. They are often the last surviving tissue on the human body.

GLASS FLASK "CONTAINING A WITCH"
THE PITT RIVERS MUSEUM, OXFORD

What is most intriguing about this artifact is that it may not contain anything at all, yet it still yields power as it has not been opened since it made its way into the Pitt Rivers Museum collection.

The specimen was collected in the field by Margaret Murray—the archaeologist famous for developing the witch cult hypothesis. The bottle is a small silver vessel with a stopper and was acquired in 1915 before being donated in 1926. The coating of the bottle in silver is intriguing, especially since silver has often been associated with supernatural beings. The vessel may contain small traces of hair, blood, or ashes given its size, but this is not mentioned anywhere—it is simply stated as "containing a witch."

The old lady who gave Murray the flask allegedly said, "They do say there be a witch in it, and if you let un out, there'll be a peck o'trouble."

The bottle has so much mystique surrounding it, and although it very well may not contain any human remains, it still seems to possess the "essence" of the fear surrounding witchcraft.

SKELETON HAND
MUSEUM OF WITCHCRAFT AND MAGIC, CORNWALL

The final object is a skeleton hand also on display in Cornwall—it has been strung together and was apparently used in casting divinations.

The use of bone magic became common in some places in the 17th Century and was, at one time, punishable by death. The hands of executed criminals were sometimes requested at the gallows, with some believing a touch of the hand could cure ailments. A Hand of Glory was often created from the dried or mummified hand of a hanged criminal or from a hand that had been amputated as a form of punishment. These types of remains were also thought to be useful against burglars or unwanted guests.

The hand itself is quite a humanizing and identifying feature of the human body. We hold the hands of the ones we love, use hands in our hobbies and work, and they are often used as a form of expression in conversation. It is no wonder they were believed to harness great power.

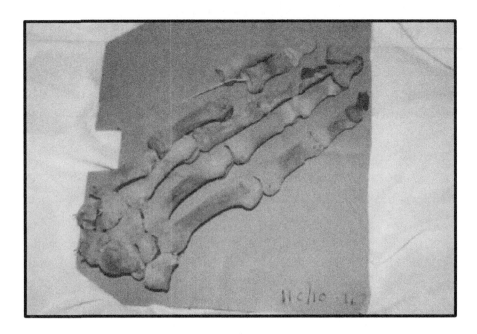

References:

Anderson, C.J., 2015. The Importance of Appearances in Literature: What Does It Mean to Be a Redhead in Literature?

Dell, C., 2016. *The occult, witchcraft & magic: an illustrated history.* Thames & Hudson.

Ebenstein, J., 2016. *The Anatomical Venus.* Thames & Hudson.

Lipscomb, S., 2018. *Witchcraft: A Ladybird Expert Book* (Vol. 36). Penguin UK.

Pickering, D., 2014. *Dictionary of Witchcraft.* David Pickering.

Ruby, J.D., Cox, C.F., Akimoto, N., Meada, N. and Momoi, Y., 2010. The caries phenomenon: a timeline from witchcraft and superstition to opinions of the 1500s to today's science. *International journal of dentistry, 2010.*

https://museumofwitchcraftandmagic.co.uk/object/charm-3/

https://museumofwitchcraftandmagic.co.uk/visit/

https://museumofwitchcraftandmagic.co.uk/object/skeletal-hand/

http://objects.prm.ox.ac.uk/pages/PRMUID25731.html

https://www.museumoflondon.org.uk/discover/sorcery-display-witch-bottles#:~:text=Modern%20witch%20bottle%20found%20on%20the%20Thames%20foreshore&text=It%20was%20found%20on%20the,latest%20coin%20dates%20from%201982.

https://www.ashmolean.org/spellbound

https://www.ashmolean.org/sites/default/files/ashmolean/documents/media/spellbounds_teacher_notes.pdf

https://baystate-dental.com/teeth-in-folklore/

https://www.atlasobscura.com/articles/morbid-monday-severed-hands

Image Sources

Bernard McManus from Victoria, BC, Canada, CC BY 2.0 <https://creativecommons.org/licenses/by/2.0>, via Wikimedia Commons

https://museumofwitchcraftandmagic.co.uk/object/skeletal-hand/

https://museumofwitchcraftandmagic.co.uk/object/charm-3/

https://www.museumoflondon.org.uk/discover/sorcery-display-witch-bottles#:~:text=Modern%20witch%20bottle%20found%20on%20the%20Thames%20foreshore&text=It%20was%20found%20on%20the,latest%20coin%20dates%20from%201982.

https://www.museumoflondon.org.uk/discover/sorcery-display-witch-bottles

My Summer of Sam:
Letters to David Berkowitz

Amelia Cotter

TRIGGER WARNING: THIS ARTICLE MENTIONS MURDER, MASS SHOOTINGS, AND RAPE.

It began in 2019 with *Conversations with a Killer: The Ted Bundy Tapes*. I was aware of the assertion that Ted Bundy was charming, flirtatious, and one of the few serial killers who was alluring and irresistible to women. When I watched the show with my husband Jonathan, we remarked that the folks primarily referring to Bundy as "charming" were other men. Bundy's longtime girlfriend, Elizabeth Kloepfer, suspected he was a killer long before he was arrested and long before he was permitted to strut around a courtroom without handcuffs, flaunting his law school prowess while the judge lamented his lost future as a lawyer.

Judge Edward Cowart sentenced Bundy to death in 1979 with the words, "You'd have made a good lawyer. I'd have loved to have you practice in front of me. But you went the wrong way, partner. Take care of yourself." Similar words have echoed from the mouths of judges in recent sexual assault cases—strangely worded sentiments that seem to imply it's a pity to have to punish these dudes.

I then watched *Extremely Wicked, Shockingly Evil, and Vile*, the Ted Bundy movie starring Zac Efron, and was so sickened by Bundy's watered-down portrayal as attractive and smooth that I became incensed by the notion that anyone could ever find him "charming."

Ted Bundy was, without a doubt, creepy. I imagine the women he met realized this rather quickly. Bundy preyed upon women's socially coerced inclination to be polite and helpful by pretending to need help, luring women to his car for assistance, and then hitting them on the back of the head with a blunt object before they ever saw it coming. This sounds not like the acts of a debonair man about town but of a cruel and spineless coward.

> OF COURSE, IN THESE CASES, THE STORYTELLERS WEREN'T THE VICTIMS, AND SO THE LEGEND OF BUNDY'S CHARM PERSISTS.

Pondering the above and considering that Bundy indeed garnered a great deal of female fans, even marrying and fathering a child with one in prison, I was compelled to wonder how and why certain people, especially certain women, become infatuated with killers.

The desire to aid and foster prisoners—even the most violent ones—is noble, and charitable acts toward incarcerated men and women are much-needed services. Society condemns prisoners to a life of misery while also calling for prison reform and then leaving the altruism to a good-hearted minority of folks who provide books, educational opportunities, and even companionship to prisoners through care packages, letter-writing, and visits.

Somewhere in between the apathy and empathy are millions of casual true crime fans, along with the rarer and more intense dark history and horror fans, and the small but growing community of hardcore "murderabilia" collectors: people who seek out the art, artifacts, and autographs of some of society's most notorious criminals. Also, somewhere in between are a distinct group: those looking to killers for connection, love, or personal attention.

Corresponding through letters can be romantic and carried out from a safe and fantasy-worthy distance. But sometimes, women also marry their killer pen pals. And sometimes, they invest their life savings into trying to exonerate or free them. And sometimes they even bear children with them.

And to what end? What won't a girl do to feel special, am I right? What won't a woman sacrifice to help a man in need? These are glib but serious questions, leaving a lot for each of us to unpack. I'm not at liberty to judge. I'm a lifelong observer of the strange and unusual and an interpreter and storyteller for people with such experiences to share. When I encountered the level of discomfort that Ted Bundy's so-called charm caused me, I challenged myself to drag my own shadows into the light. Enter *The Sons of Sam: A Descent into Darkness* in summer 2021.

Elbow deep in pandemic restlessness, my mind was wide open to challenges and new concepts, and I found a strange hobby in all things David Berkowitz. I devoured the Netflix documentary as well as articles, books, and YouTube videos about the Son of Sam, diving all the way down the rabbit hole with journalist Maury Terry and his eerily postmodern conspiracy theories about a complex, elite network of Satan worshippers hiding under every rock, bloodthirsty for chaos, German shepherds, and our very souls. What a story, and that's not even including the traditional telling of the Son of Sam murders, which includes a talking dog commanding Berkowitz to kill. [Much to the dismay of true crime enthusiasts, this tidbit of the story was entirely made up by Berkowitz to sweeten the deal for an insanity plea, which didn't end up working out for him.]

I learned that Berkowitz was sentenced to six consecutive life sentences and is still alive and thriving in the Shawangunk Correctional Facility in Wallkill, New York, preaching his born-again Christian values as the newly christened, "Son of Hope." He's nearly 70 and has a solid reputation as an all-around nice guy who seems to have genuinely repented for his crimes and, unlike Bundy, never made a low-brow attempt at blaming them on pornography (just another sneaky way of sex-shaming and victim-blaming women).

Berkowitz seemed like Mr. Rogers compared to Bundy. Berkowitz "only" killed six and injured nine. He shot people from a distance, only twice coming in close contact with young women during two failed stabbing attempts. Bundy was suspected of killing more than 36 women, beating, biting, raping, and mutilating them in unimaginable ways. I, for one, haven't killed anybody, but felt less abhorred by Berkowitz's crimes for some reason.

I was particularly interested in the story of Berkowitz's treatment during and after his trial. He was harassed and ridiculed for being an outsider, loner, and virgin. His personal and social life, in fact, suggested otherwise, at least as far as being a total loser. The strong likelihood of him having paranoid schizophrenia also became the butt of cultural jokes for decades to come, denigrating hundreds of thousands of people with the disease who are neither "crazy" nor a danger to society.

Taking Berkowitz's crimes out of the picture for a moment, I found the underpinning messages around these killers clear: young men convicted of sexual assault are considered an unfortunate loss to society, young men who might be virgins are fodder for laughter and scorn, and young women who might not be virgins—and are often victims—ultimately get what's coming to them.

Bundy has historically been seen as captivating, charming, and even virile for being smart, evading police, and attacking women with full force. At the same time, Berkowitz was viewed as timid, sheepish, and even impotent for firing his gun at people from a distance.

Oh, the humanity.

I began to see a reflection of American machoism along with gender and sexual politics in these men and our cultural interactions with their stories. I also found myself reflecting. Bundy was wicked and vile to me indeed, but Berkowitz seemed like… an okay guy? Did I just feel sorry for him? Was my brain searching for a shred of familiarity and understanding, or a piece of myself somewhere in the story? Was I angry at Bundy for being a charming asshole, or was I angry at the world for equating asshole behavior with *charm*?

I could go on for many more pages asking many more questions, and I don't really have answers. All I know is that I couldn't look away, couldn't get enough, and couldn't stop thinking about it, all while circling back to one simple, weird fact: there was something about Berkowitz that I just *liked*. He had grown on me, whether I wanted him to or not. I was beginning to understand how some people, especially women grappling with bigger issues around abuse recovery, traumatic memories, and toxic masculinity, might have a series of thoughts leading to a series of smaller and then bigger choices in their exploration of killer culture.

I decided to scratch the painful itch of morbid curiosity and guilty fascination by doing the very thing I couldn't believe anyone would want to do in the first place: I wrote Berkowitz a letter. If you can't beat 'em, join 'em… or something like that.

I sent him a handwritten letter asking basic questions about how he was doing and mentioning that I had seen the documentary and just wanted to reach out and acknowledge his humanity. I excessively researched the rules of writing to someone in prison and located an out-of-the-way mailbox in the neighborhood where no one would see me nervously drop the letter. I wondered what the folks at the U.S. Postal Service would think of me for sending it and waited about two months.

One day in late summer, Jonathan burst through the front door holding a handful of mail and asked breathlessly, "Did you write a letter to an inmate? Uh, you got a letter from David Berkowitz." My heart jumped into my throat. I had opted not to tell Jonathan about my new pen pal because I feared his judgment. I'm self-aware enough to know it was a wild thing to do, but also figured if Berkowitz wrote back, it would make my actions seem somehow less weird and maybe even kind of cool. Jonathan was certainly impressed by my commitment to my "hobbies," and when we opened and read Berkowitz's response, typed out with precision on his classic electric

typewriter, seeing his signature on the back of the letter was truly an arresting sight. And it was, indeed, cool.

Berkowitz's response was cordial and polite. He talked a little about COVID and about receiving hundreds of extra letters because of the Netflix documentary. He reminded me to have faith in God and sent me some propaganda about his journey to redemption and salvation through Christ. It was friendly and distant, and (thankfully) not an invitation to be his girlfriend, or even to write back. Berkowitz has done his part in recent years to assist in stopping the spread of the "murderabilia" industry, so I was surprised he was willing to hand-sign the letter at all. Maybe he sensed I'm not the type to write to serial killers, or perhaps I just need to reassure myself that I'm not.

But I didn't exactly stop there. I sent him a Christmas card, too. I figured sending an additional correspondence would make me seem less like a fetishist, considering the number of people who, like me, suddenly felt entitled to reach out to a person with nowhere to hide from thrill-seekers begging for attention, even if just for the span of a letter. In my mind, a Christmas card solidified my integrity and good faith.

I didn't expect another response, didn't receive one, and felt satisfied with our interaction. In a way, it helped me heal some traumatic memories. Receiving a kind word from someone who was once extremely unkind redeemed my belief that people can change, including those who have hurt me. It encouraged me to empathize (even if only a little) with people we consider evil or irredeemable. I'm glad I decided to stop when I did, but I can also see how some people wouldn't.

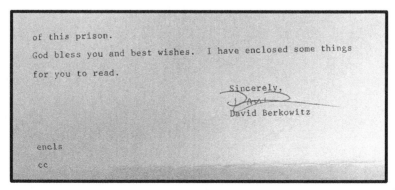

of this prison.
God bless you and best wishes. I have enclosed some things
for you to read.

Sincerely,
David Berkowitz

encls
cc

My fascination with this topic continues, but with the hope of creating meaningful and timely discourse around the many sub-themes it generates. I wish to be sensitive to the exploitation of the feelings, experiences, and stories of those who aren't here to speak for themselves. I also wish to be mindful of the parallel issue of mass shootings and the abhorrent culture of apologism surrounding mass shooters. I struggled with whether it should be appropriate to try and address them here, in the context of romantic fascination with killer culture, and I want to make sure I at least acknowledge the bigger picture.

Memes about the dark history and true crime genres suggest they provide us with "comfort" while addressing the uncomfortable. They allow for a broader glimpse not only into those who perpetrate acts of unimaginable cruelty, but also our *reactions* to them—vital, revealing, and important responses from which we cannot, and should not, look away.

THEIR STORIES ARE TOLD IN BRANCHES AND BONES

Gina Armstrong and

Victoria Vancek

Every community has at least one. They can be subtle and unsuspecting, even tucked away and somewhat obscured. Others can be grandiose, populous, and capture the eye. Some can simply evoke that childhood feeling of foreboding and dread. They are graveyards and cemeteries.

There is something innately haunting and eerily beautiful about cemeteries. Stoic monuments dot and tower above quiet, green grounds. By day cemeteries are peaceful, relaxing, and parklike. Then twilight moves in, and nightfall meticulously folds over the landscape. The ambiance transforms to unveil looming headstones, twisted tree branches, and flitting shadows.

> ## THESE SACRED PLACES ARE MUSEUMS FOR THE DEAD.

Past lives of souls mingle in such a place, so it is fitting that many of us are drawn to where so many fascinating stories lie left untold. For historians, taphophiles, and paranormal researchers, cemeteries are like time capsules waiting to be opened—figuratively speaking, of course!

Those of us who love cemeteries wander about, straining to read the often worn and moss-covered chiseled markers. We can almost hear far away ethereal voices hanging in the wind to gently remind us of the steady passing of time. Like puzzle pieces, we can trace the history of grave markers and use the stories we unearth to fill in missing or unknown parts of history.

Grave markers and their symbols function as great storytellers and can teach us much about the history of an era. While it's natural to focus on the dead in a cemetery, it is the living in a burial site that you might notice the next time you pay a visit—namely, flowers, shrubs, and particularly the magnificent trees.

Cemetery trees, like sentinels, continuously watching silently and patiently over the departed, offer intriguing stories. These guardians of the dead are portals bearing fascinating symbolic significance. Trees and shrubs absorb the energies in their environment, and though they may appear to be growing haphazardly, that is not always the case. Many are planted for specific reasons— personal, religious, or cultural. Cemetery flora folklore offers valuable insight into what people of certain eras believed and why specific trees became part of the cemetery landscape.

Once loosely based on folklore or religious beliefs, practices of growing and the placement of certain trees and shrubs in cemeteries are still adopted and survive today. Myths and legends associated with trees share ties to human spirituality and superstitions. This is found across all cultures—some relate to the lands where the trees or shrubs originated. Occasionally specific trees were planted in cemeteries providing familiarity to new settlers. When it comes to funerary art, flora (specifically trees) has

Cemetery landscapes are still based on folklore and symbolism.

harkened back to ancient times over a span of centuries.

So, while tombstones are the main focus in a cemetery, the majestic trees are enthralling monuments that offer a plentitude of richly enchanting narratives.

CYPRESS

The cypress is a classic graveyard tree that grows worldwide in a vast array of climates.

It is believed that the cross used in the crucifixion of Jesus was made from cypress wood and, as such, has become a symbol of eternity. Ancient Greeks would place the ashes of soldiers who died in battle inside urns made from cypress wood. The tree became associated with death and the underworld because when cut too severely, it fails to regenerate. The cypress became popular in ancient Muslim and European cultures and is still widely planted as the tree of choice in cemeteries.

Cypress trees were regarded as gloomy symbols of sorrow. Burnaby Masonic Cemetery, British Columbia

Celtic mourners would place their dearly departed inside the trees themselves for burials. The tree's appearance often described as dark and gloomy, inspired people to plant them in cemeteries to express sorrow and mourning. They would often plant a cypress near a grave to denote the presence of a corpse. The sturdy needles of the tree, unfettered by wind or harsh weather, were said to represent an individual who preserved his unwavering virtue even in death.

MONKEY PUZZLE

One particular cemetery tree with a unique superstition is the Monkey Puzzle. An exotic native found on the cordillera of the Andes Mountains of Chile and Argentina dates back to antiquity. The Mapuche tribes of south-central Chile and southwestern Argentina believed the Monkey Puzzle tree to be steeped with sacred qualities long before it was introduced to other countries. The Monkey Puzzle family can be traced back to the Mesozoic Era (250 million years ago).

It is believed the spiky leaves evolved to deter grazing dinosaurs. Its ability to grow 30-40 meters tall and live for 1,000 years makes this an ideal cemetery tree representing longevity. In the 19th Century, British superstitions around the Monkey Puzzle came about by parents as a warning to prevent children from playing around or climbing the spiky branches. Parents would tell their children if they were not silent "whilst walking past the tree," they'd be unlucky, lose something precious to them, or in some cases even grow a monkey's tail!

Monkey Puzzle trees are said to be a perch for the Devil. Fraser Cemetery, New Westminster, BC.

Another common folktale is that the Devil would perch in the tree awaiting anyone passing by. From this, an old Cambridgeshire belief originated that Monkey Puzzle trees should be planted along the outermost edges of cemeteries and graveyards. This would prevent the Devil from climbing the tree to watch fresh burials and attempt to steal the souls of the departed.

CAMPERDOWN ELM

According to Germanic mythology, the Camperdown Elm is called "Embla," an ancient name representing the first woman born. In Celtic cultures, ancient Druid priests associated the elm with female divinity. This stately tree was said to have psychic powers that could foretell the future. It is also the tree of dreams, sleep, and death. Various superstitions and myths are linked to the elm by different cultures. The Knights Templar viewed the elm as an oracle and would add the phrase "of the Elm" at the end of the title of their church's name.

Camperdown Elms—symbols of female divinity, dreams, and death. Ross Bay Cemetery, Victoria, BC.

In French mythology, the elm is "the tree of justice" and was believed to instill the power of intuition and clear vision. It was under this tree that judges would receive inspiration for sentencing. With many similar symbolic connotations over diverse cultures, it's not a wonder that the elm is revered as a magical tree.

In Victorian times, elm leaves were made into beds for children to strengthen their bones, and in cemeteries, Camperdown Elms can often be found planted near children's graves. Also called the "umbrella tree" for its unusual weeping formation and dense foliage, it was highly sought-after in Victorian cemeteries as a symbol of protection against evil and chaos. In Celtic mythology, elm trees were connected to elves—not only watching over their dead and burial mounds but also as guardians of those passing into the Underworld.

YEW

Evergreens such as yew trees long existed as symbols of the regeneration of the natural world and the spirit. Yews were considered to have magical properties and, in pagan cultures, were planted near temples and sacred spaces for centuries. Why yew trees are planted in graveyards stems from the symbolism of the trees themselves. The evergreen nature of the tree has historically been a metaphor for the body's resurrection and the soul's immortality. It is believed that this representation made them an appropriate tree to give hope in a graveyard.

Pagan religions were gradually replaced with Christianity, but the tree remains a steadfast feature in cemeteries.

As far as practicality regarding cemetery landscapes, the yew, like many other cemetery trees, can live a very long time. Unobstructed in a cemetery, unlike a densely populated forest, yews can flourish without competition and live for an inordinately long time. Suggestions have been made that yews can live for thousands of years. As a

Yew trees were symbols of immortality. Ross Bay Cemetery, Victoria, BC.

result, a vibrant tapestry of folklore surrounds this ancient tree.

The most macabre reason for the yew being planted in cemeteries was the belief that the twisted roots would grow far-reaching under the soil, eventually entwining through the eye sockets of the dead to prevent them from rising again.

CEDAR

When it comes to a funerary connection, the lofty cedar tree has been used in death rituals as far back as the Egyptians, who used cedar resin to mummify their dead. Indigenous peoples like the Cherokee or the Kwakwaka'wakw regarded the cedar as "the tree of life." Many parts of the Red Cedar tree—wood, berries, leaves, and bark were used for medicinal purposes in treating such ailments as cough, bronchitis, and joint pain. The Cherokee believed that cedars held the spirits of their departed. The Salish consider the tree to represent generosity and protection.

Cedar trees were said to keep the dead contained. Christ Church Cemetery, Surrey, BC.

The cedar is often referred to as "the graveyard tree," and though they are common in cemeteries, Ozark folklore warns that you do not want a cedar tree to shade the burial plot where you will eventually be interred. If the tree casts a shadow on your future resting place, you'll die sooner rather than later. Thank goodness these trees take a very long time to grow! Also, if one tries to relocate a cedar tree and it dies, one is said to follow the same fate soon after.

Throughout history, the cedar has been used in healing, purification, and spiritual protection. It is said to drive out negative energy and bring in positive influences. Even the Bible mentions cedars as part of ritual cleansing.

For pragmatic reasons, the tree is used in many graveyards—the shallow root system makes it a great candidate for cemetery landscapes. Roots won't grow out of control and interfere with burial plots, yet the tree is tall and sturdy to protect cemetery landscapes from harsh weather. Often cedar trees are used as a natural boundary around a cemetery instead of a man-made fence because many species grow upright and can be kept easily manicured. Going back in time, cedar barriers were planted in much the same way. However, the reasons for the trees encircling a graveyard were for far more than just practical reasons. Cedar trees as barriers were thought to keep the spirits of the dead firmly contained.

OAK

In major cultures worldwide, the oak tree was historically held in high regard. The Druids often performed their rites in oak groves, while among Greeks, Romans, Celts, and Slavs, the oak was associated with powerful gods. Oak trees have a high water content and are very prone to lightning strikes if they are the tallest thing in a landscape. Attracting lightning led to all sorts of mythology about various gods who had dominion over thunder, lightning, and rainfall. Because of a connection to weather, a more recent Irish rhyme says:

If the oak before the ash,
Then we'll only have a splash.
If the ash before the oak,
Then we'll surely have a soak!

Much of the spiritual appreciation of the oak may be due to its size and presence. One of the earliest records of the oak being a symbol associated with death is connected to Leicestershire Park, where The Topless Oaks in Bradgate Park are a symbol of mourning as a result of the beheading of Lady Jane Grey in 1554, who lived nearby.

Not only are oak trees planted in cemeteries, but oak leaves and acorns have adorned tombstones for centuries. The fact that such an impressive tree can grow from a single acorn became a symbol of greatness arising from humble beginnings. The oak is symbolic of strength, protection, endurance, and eternity.

Children's graves were often placed near oak trees. Christ Church Cemetery, Surrey, BC.

In smaller pioneer cemeteries, it's common to place children's graves near an oak tree. The oak was regarded as a tree of life in pre-Christian times, and this sentiment still carries over to the modern day. A cemetery's somber landscape of dark evergreens is made more welcoming by the grandeur of a leafy green oak tree which also provides large areas of shade for visitors.

WILLOW

A single tree branch from the willow, if planted into the ground, will produce a new tree. This trait alone has the tree associated with renewal and immortality.

A wand made of willow is said to embody a number of magical qualities. In Scotland, people sometimes made a three-ply cord from the parts of the tree to protect from hostile, unseen forces. The Greek poet Orpheus carried willow branches on his adventures into the Underworld, and the ancient Chinese believed that willow branches would ward off evil spirits. Willows have long inspired myths and legends in every culture. Where they grow, they are an important tree for ancient peoples, including those of Egypt, Greece, China, and the Celts. They also figure into many fairy tales.

During the 16th and 17th Centuries, weeping willows became associated with grief and suffering.

By the 19th Century, illustrations of willow trees appeared on gravestones and mourning cards. In cemeteries, the willow became a symbol of life after death, resilience, and vitality. Wearing willow branches as a talisman would speed up the healing process after an individual experienced an unfortunate end. These attributes and the tree's graceful, bowed shape made it a standard fixture in the cemetery landscape. Willows are long associated with being the "tree of ghosts," and it is said the tree can evoke souls and touch a ghost.

Weeping willows were said to be able to touch ghosts. Mennonite Cemetery, Abbotsford, BC.

Cemeteries and graveyards have historically brought about a uniquely dark allure due to tales of hauntings, strange occurrences, or ethereal residents. At the same time, they can be a great escape from the daily hectic paces, and you don't need to exit your earthly life to be a patron. While large park-like cemeteries often attract their share of visitors, don't overlook smaller tucked-away graveyards that are off the beaten path, a bit overgrown, humble, and sometimes unnoticed.

Where human history and natural history meet.

Burial locations—large or small—gather strong energies and emotions over centuries and, within their mysterious serenity, offer up their gifts of historic information. Whether it's to visit a loved one, take a reflective nature walk, or commune with the dead, a cemetery can be a great place to wander. These sacred spaces hold great historical and natural value, not to be overlooked by those who enjoy a good graveyard.

As twilight seeps through the tree branches, we find stillness, captivating stories, and perhaps a ghostly sighting. Meandering contemplatively in a graveyard, we might question how we, the living, can share a truly spiritual moment in such a place with those who have passed on. If we pay attention, we realize cemeteries are truly places of magic. They are places where human history and natural history are woven together.

While some of us attempt to communicate with the dead using verbal cues or through electronic equipment, cemeteries offer their own unique conduits to the dead. Among the grave markers, we inhale the scent of springtime flowers and hear the rustle of leaves whispering in the wind. While gravestones sit stationary in their silent presence, we witness seasons change in a flower, a shrub, or a tree. Here we are reminded of the transience of life.

> A NEVER-ENDING CYCLE LIVES IN THE PLACE WHERE THE DEAD RESIDE. EVIDENT IN A PURE, SIMPLE EVENT SUCH AS THE ANNUAL GROWTH OF A TREE.

For one seemingly timeless moment, an exalting experience between the otherworldly and the living converges. A tangible, unspoken shared connection manifests and is captured within the beauteous, mystical realms of Nature.

> *"It was probably the last stone surviving…*
> *Nothing else was left,*
> *Only a fountain and a tree."*
>
> -*The Canal Garden*,
> Jaroslav Seifert

To Walk Between the Worlds

Renee Bedard

I take a deep breath in and slowly let it out. The early morning light dances through the trees, creating slippery shapes upon the screen of my closed eyelids. I wonder, "Are they shadows or spirits?" A smile appears on my lips. With reverence, I ask permission to enter the forest. "I wish to walk as a witch among the many spirits of such a beautiful place. I hope to commune and strengthen my connection between the realm of the spirits and the living if you will allow me."

A breeze picks up, allowing the faint whispers to embrace me. There is a cool tingle upon my skin. It is quite the contrast with the warm sun. In my heart, I feel my answer. "Welcome, witch."

As gratitude pours from my heart, I offer water at the trailhead. "Thank you, spirits. I am happy to be back."

For me, one of the aspects of a witch is to commune with the gods, spirits, energies, and beings all around me. To see, feel, speak, *and* listen, experience, and partner with the spirit world doesn't just help us gain a greater understanding of the world around us and our place in it—it opens a multilayered reality where we can help and be helped, heal and be healed, learn and teach, and see and be seen. When I pause for a moment to feel the environment in the physical world, I am feeling more than the world around me and my place in it.

> I PAUSE TO FEEL MY THREAD THAT IS INTERLACED WITHIN THE TAPESTRY OF LIFE.

This allows me to recognize all the other threads woven together so we can experience and interact with the beautiful work of art we call life.

As a witch, this is how I see life all around me. Everything is alive and connected. This energy is vital to creating everything in the world, both seen and unseen. Because of these intricate connections, I believe there is potential for a partnership between the witch and the spirits that want to work with us. By recognizing a spirit's presence and autonomy, we open a doorway for communication and understanding. When we ask for permission to enter a space that is not ours, it shows them that we respect and honor their presence, space, world, and sovereignty. As a result, we may make a new ally. However, if we receive a no to enter an area as a witch, I would take caution and honor the denied request.

Witches hold the mantle of "a walker between the worlds." That means a witch lives and works with one foot in the physical realm and the other moving in the realm of the spirits. When a witch works with spirits or entities, be it goddesses and gods, ancestors, nature spirits, or the various other types of beings and energies, they can consciously move from the physical realm into the spirit realm and back again at will. We purposefully walk in service to those in both realms, acting as a bridge between the worlds. It is our duty to assist and support where we are needed. It is also rewarding and comforting to receive help from the spirit world when we may be in need. That is why beneficial partnerships are necessary. It is part of our work as a witch and carries a tremendous responsibility that we must be prepared to honor and practice in our daily lives.

Spirits are everywhere. There are layers upon layers of those that came before us, both human and inhuman, creating countless lessons to uncover. Witches can tap into this vast library of knowledge to help make the change we need or desire. The spirit world is all around us. By learning how to understand the energies that weave around us every day, we can transform that knowledge into the wisdom we need as we travel into the spaces where we do not physically dwell. With respectful and conscientious effort, we can build a team of helpful spirits to aid us on our journey. These spirit guides can act as our teachers, advisors, mentors, protectors, emissaries, or even ambassadors of our will. They also help us with the needs of others and ourselves, be it healing, releasing, teaching, or learning.

So, where do we begin our work? To be a walker between the worlds can sound very romantic and even powerful. This is especially true since there is a lot of pressure to create catchy soundbites emphasizing appealing aesthetics. What the title means is that there is a lot of dedication and hard work to be done through study and daily practice.

> A WITCH MUST BE ABLE TO BE GROUNDED WITHIN THEMSELVES AND WHO THEY ARE.

Experiences on this path can be very subjective in the spirit world and even dangerous. A witch must discern a true interaction from a deep-seated longing or personal desired outcome. That is no easy feat, even for those who have been practicing for a very long time. That is why I have found it helpful to journal about everything from my personal experiences, emotions, goals, hopes, fears, biases, successes, and failures. The more we understand who we are, the more we can understand the world around us and those in it, both corporeal and non-corporeal.

I find this to be true for witches and non-witches alike. Knowledge is power. This is especially true when it comes to ourselves. What are the motives behind your actions? Are you seeking hard, cold truth or personal truth? Are you searching for answers or for something to fit your narrative? These are not easy questions to answer, nor are they revealed easily. However, the journey you take upon this road of self-discovery is a journey well worth the reflection. It will help you peel away the subjectiveness of your own personal perspective. With honest, diligent, and dedicated work, you will be granted an objective view that would probably be better than any outcome you may have imagined for yourself. This is the work of the witch. It will help strengthen healthy spirit partnerships. Hopefully, it is what also grants the hard-earned trust and respect of our guides in the spiritual realm.

I have mentioned that this work requires daily practice. This is true for many reasons. It is essential to check in on our friends and loved ones that physically surround us in our daily lives. It is how we show our love, concern, and respect for them. We care about them and wish them health, happiness, and love. If we are needed, we find a way to help them in their time of need. We try our best to be a good friend and partner. This is true for the spirits we commune with as well. They also have needs, goals, and concerns. They walk a path in spirit that requires care, friendship, and at times, a helping hand. To have partners in the spirit world is just like having partners in the physical world. Friendships need to be fostered with time, energy, and respect—whether they have a physical body or not. That is why checking in on your guides, or spirit team as some call them, is vital. The partnership must be reciprocal. We assist each other in our work. Offering the spirits your time, candles, water, herbs, food, alcohol, and even energy is important. It shows them we care and appreciate their time, effort, and friendship. If the relationship is one-sided, the spirits may not come forward when we call them, just as we would experience similar results with a living person.

> **THESE PARTNERSHIPS ARE REAL. THEY NEED TO BE FED AND TAKEN CARE OF FOR THEM TO GROW.**

When we understand that and nurture our friends and connections, we find they are truly powerful and beneficial allies in all aspects of our lives. Personally, I like to leave offerings for specific allies on certain days. This helps me to keep my steady practice moving. Checking in with my team to chat in a quiet space or meditation is also helpful. It gives me a chance to understand where I am in the present moment. I can seek insight into what my next step may be. When I request council, it can be for things like healing or to point me in a helpful direction. My guides have been working with me for a long time, and I am grateful for them and our friendship.

THE WORKINGS OF A WITCH

The work of the witch has many different facets. It will vary from witch to witch. We do not have a set of rules or strict dogma that we must abide by. Each witch works their own Will and is called to work in their own way [The "w" is capitalized to represent our Divine Will]. We are our own emissaries when working with the spirit world. There is no "middle person" that we must rely on. We are the ones who reach out to the spirits from the physical plane. It is our job as witches to bridge the two worlds together to gain a deeper understanding of everything around us as we strive for harmony. It is beautiful and rewarding work as well as tricky and challenging.

For my personal work, I want to understand the worlds around me and explore the connections that we share. If there is something that I can assist with, I am happy to help the spirit or energy in need if they are accepting of it. I love to go to places where I can feel the area's history, sink my roots into the land, and explore it psychically, energetically, and through my five physical senses. I want to peel back the layers of patterns created through the centuries and witness the countless stories lost through the passage of time. I can explore these lost worlds by going to established and unknown "haunted" locations. It gives me a chance to work with my spirit team in a place that I am unfamiliar. This is another reason why it is crucial to work well with your spirit guides. Calling them in to assist with this work is incredibly helpful. They walk with me and keep me safe while we are together. They guard the gates for me while I am communing with the spirits of a place, creating a buffer zone around me. I trust my guides during these sessions. They are much better at the spirit world than I am. With their guidance, knowledge, and protection, I can safely work in an unknown environment when I am listening to what they say… if the location permits me to do so. I also must heed their warning when it is time for me to go because I know it is for my own safety.

Each destination has its own personality. Some locations can have years and even centuries of thoughts, expectations, legends, and creative myths imposed upon them. It can build an energy that takes on a life of its own. This can be true for a battlefield, a closed hospital, or even in your own home. As humans, it is easy to jump to the scary assumption. Fear and anticipation of the unknown can play tricks on us and cause us to come to the darkest conclusion. Reactive responses are usually because we have a preconceived expectation or do not understand something. We are typically afraid of the unknown, which is a normal human response. If we thought about a "haunted" location, could it be possible that the living beings are leaving imprints of their own fear at the site? I feel that is possible. Each day we understand more how our emotions and experiences create energies that can build up and linger in a space, taking on a life of their own. We know that thoughts are things.

> ISN'T IT POSSIBLE THAT WE ARE CREATING AN ENERGY THAT IS HAUNTING US?

This is why we must work hard to understand who we are and what biases we may hold.

I like to go to quieter places while doing my private work. The places that may be off the map, so to speak. I have found that there is less "energetic clutter" that I must cut through to get to the heart of a location. As a result, it is easier for me to enter without expectation. Besides, spirits are everywhere. I like to visit places I can explore and hopefully make contact with those on the other side who have a story to tell or may need assistance. In my experience, those are the places where I have a more profound and more powerful interaction. Without knowledge of the recorded activity, I am less likely to subconsciously make my experiences fit the location's reputation or mythology. When

I connect with the genius loci, the spirit of place, it is possible to feel each other's energy and begin to commune objectively. I will always introduce myself and explain why I am there. Sometimes it's because I have been drawn there. It could be a dream, a call from a spirit upon that land, or simply a longing to go there. If I am granted permission to walk as a witch, a walker between the worlds, there is usually a wonderful exchange of information and energy in these spaces. As a result, I have made some wonderful allies. There have even been some instances where the spirits of certain places have reached out to me through my guides, asking me to come back so we can work together again. I am happy to do so.

Every situation is different. Every location has a unique set of factors to make it what it is. To be a walker between the worlds is to understand the delicate balance in every space. We must allow the living and those in spirit to be heard. Respect and kindness can go a very long way. By entering a location, we want to recognize and honor that point for all involved. That way, we can move forward with a well-informed set of facts with harmony as the outcome.

I believe that there is magick all around us. Walking between the worlds, I am reminded of this simple truth daily. Between the beauty and mystery of the physical and spirit worlds, magick is endless. My desire to understand energy and spirits has benefited my work as a witch, psychic, healer, mentor, and priestess. It helps me to be a better human. I am allowed to see life through a broader, more objective lens. I have been nudged to look outside the box for solutions to problems. I am challenged to explore different avenues that may seem a little out of the ordinary. I have found a true treasure when unexpected answers arrive. When I am allowed to hold a sacred space, I listen to what the spirits and humans say. Deep and powerful connections are made when I let the situation unfold without my anticipated or expected assumptions. Through this work, I have witnessed reconnections with loved ones that have passed over. Healing wounds between family members and couples can occur when the intense energy between them is released and room for love is made in their hearts. Helping a loved one's transition from the physical to the spirit world is never easy, but peace is found within that work.

Being a walker between the worlds can be difficult sometimes, yet the rewards are greater than I have ever imagined. I wholeheartedly feel that the work of the witch is a calling. It is my calling. It is a calling to serve those on both sides of the veil. It is a calling to witness each and every soul and entity that has graced this planet throughout time as they are. We all have a desire to be seen.

> WE WANT TO FEEL THAT OUR LIFE MATTERS AND THAT OUR WORK WAS NOT IN VAIN.

We hope that our efforts will live on after we die. I am grateful to have the ability and opportunity to walk this path as I strive to embody the principle of perfect love and perfect trust. I cannot imagine my life any other way. I am a witch. I am a walker between the worlds. Magick is alive and well within us all. Maybe it is waiting for us to realize that it has been there all along.

Beyond the Bride: How Varying Finalities of Death in *Bride of Frankie* Complicate the *Frankenstein* Genre's Approach to Gender

Rebecca Gibson

In the 2017 short film *Bride of Frankie*, filmmaker Devi Snively reimagines *Frankenstein* through a feminist lens, and gives the viewer a deeper interpretation of death and its permanency. In Mary Shelley's original novel (1818/1831), one theme that repeats throughout is that of "playing god," and how Victor Frankenstein's creation, once released, takes on a life of his own. Spurned by his creator, outcast by society, and physically and existentially miserable, the creature becomes violent. *Bride of Frankie* seeks to answer the question— what if the creature were given love, attention, affection, and kindness? What kind of life would they choose to lead? And knowing that, in this instance, death is a door that swings both ways, how might they choose to die?

Before beginning my analysis of *Bride of Frankie*, however, I will refresh the reader on the various iterations of the *Frankenstein* myth seen on the large and small screen. To put it

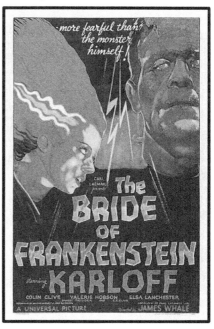

briefly, there are a lot—many more than are at first obvious via their titles or subject matter. In addition to the standard retellings (*Frankenstein* [Whale, 1931]; *Bride of Frankenstein* [Whale, 1935]; *Re-animator* [Gordon, 1985]), there are the comedic ones (*Young Frankenstein* [Brooks, 1974]; *Frankenhooker* [Henenlotter, 1990]; *Frankenweenie* [Burton, 2012]), and the non-standard, yet still wholly derivative "man plays god" stories, where we can see the fingerprints of Mary Shelley's masterpiece.

These derivatives can be divided into several sub-categories—selected examples of which I have listed parenthetically:

1) creator and humanoid creation (*The Skin I Live In* [Almodóvar, 2011]; *Black Mirror: Be Right Back* [Season 2, Episode 1] [Harris, 2013]; *Blade Runner* [Scott, 1982]; *Blade Runner 2049* [Villeneuve, 2017]; *The Rocky Horror Picture Show* [Sharman, 1975])

2) creator and self as creation (*The Fly* [Cronenberg, 1986]; *Lucy* [Besson, 2014]; *The Maker* [Kezelos, 2012])

3) creator and robot creation (*Ex Machina* [Garland, 2014]; *Alita: Battle Angel* [Rodriguez, 2019]; *Star Trek: The Next Generation: Datalore* [Bowman, 1988])

4) retellings of Pygmalion and Galatea (*My Fair Lady* [Cukor, 1964]; *Clueless* [Heckerling, 1995]; *We Need to Talk About Kevin* [Ramsay, 2011])

5) creator and cyborg creation (*Star Wars* [Lucas, 1977] [re: Darth Vader]; *RoboCop* [Verhoeven, 1987])

6) creator and part animal creation (*Splice* [Natali, 2009]; the *Alien* franchise after *Alien 3* [Fincher, 1992])

7) allegorical retellings (*The Spirit of the Beehive* [Erice, 1973]; *Pan's Labyrinth* [del Toro, 2006])

With a few notable exceptions, the creations on which the films and TV episodes focus are singular—or sequential—with only one existing at a time. They have no companions, no siblings, and no romantic partners of their own kind, relying on human interactions as their only social outlet. While they were once human, they are no longer, and they live lonely, misunderstood lives, un-comforted by a loving touch. However, within the above categories, one can make a further distinction: stories where the creation is meant to live a long and happy life, and ones where it is reviled by the human population.

That distinction forms a rather underpopulated category—the happy creation. While some of the creations live long lives (Ash in *Black Mirror: Be Right Back* and Ava in *Ex Machina*, for example), these lives cannot be said to be happy. Ash, a human replica android meant as a comfort-being after the human-Ash died, becomes the epitome of the Uncanny Valley by being human enough to be pitiable, thus avoiding being killed, but eerily not quite human enough to live out in public where his owner's friends and family would meet him. He spends his life locked in the attic, visited only a few times a year by his erstwhile fiancée and "their" daughter. His life is long, but emotionless on his part and filled with awkward embarrassment on the part of his owner/creator. Ava, a humanoid robot—the creation of a god-like genius—kills her maker, traps her lover in a house with no access to food, and escapes to the outside world. She is ostensibly happy at the end of the movie, but several (unexplored) possibilities exist to stymie that happiness, including a lack of charging ports for her technology, and the possibility that she will be found out, captured, experimented on, and disassembled. These feelings of happiness (or the simulation thereof in Ash's case) are *despite* the humans in their lives, not because of or with them, and the viewer understands that the downfall that stems from misunderstandings and persecutions always lurks just offscreen, ready to occur should someone find out the secret of the creation's non-human nature.

The happiest stories come from the fourth group, retellings of Pygmalion and Galatea (though an exception is *We Need to Talk About Kevin*). The original myth, briefly, centers around the creator as a sculptor, breathing life into their creation. In *My Fair Lady*, for example, the creator is Dr. Henry Higgins— a metaphorical sculptor in the form of a linguistics professor. The creation is Eliza Doolittle, a poor and dirt-covered cockney woman. Her transformation from an uncultured waif to society

darling can be seen as happy—or at least happier than most of the stories—she lives, gains social ground, is transformed, and seems happy. However, is she?

> TRANSFORMATION IS INEVITABLE IN LIFE. BUT SHE DID NOT ASK TO BE TRANSFORMED. IT WAS DONE AS AN EXPERIMENT.

Furthermore, stories that retell this myth generally involve beautiful and alive creations—they do not deal with the grotesque or the undead. *My Fair Lady* would have had different implications entirely had the star been someone less stunningly beautiful than Audrey Hepburn—the transformation was possible because the beauty was underneath the dirt and accented speech the whole time. While these stories are related to the Frankenstein mythos, they do not address my main premise: that it may be possible for an undead grotesque to defy the sad limited existence of the Frankenstein mythos if given care, compassion, love, and positive attention.

The final category of long-lived creatures can be found in comedies. *Young Frankenstein* and the like give their creations relatively happy lives beyond redemption. However, these are clearly played for laughs, with outlandish circumstances, ridiculous premises, and tongues very firmly in cheeks. In *Young Frankenstein*, the creature's brain gets a boost from his creator, so he can suddenly speak fluent English, persuading the townspeople to stop attacking him. He becomes "normal" and alive-ish, instead of "abnormal" (or "Abby Normal") and undead, thus being able to integrate into society (and a sexual relationship with his bride, Elizabeth) rather than continuing a monstrous and outcast existence. Where are the creations who are abnormal, undead, and yet still happy and long-lived? Before answering that question, we must examine why the creature must suffer in the *Frankenstein* story.

TWO ACTS OF CREATION:
BRIDE OF FRANKIE AND MARY SHELLEY'S METACOMMENTARY

The ideas of the sex and gender binaries are played out in multiple ways in various *Frankenstein* derivatives, and some stories do deviate from strictly binary characters, making the creations amorphous, non-gender-differentiated, non-sexed, or re-creating them into configurations that combine body parts into non-standard configurations. However, this is not done as an exploration of the variation of the human gender and sex spectrums, but as a means of emphasizing the non-human/inhuman nature of the creations and their disconnection with normal and natural humanity. The creations may desire companionship, but the creators desire creation as a process. And while the creations are occasionally given a partner (the eponymous Bride of Frankenstein), these are often an afterthought, serving the story and plot more than they do the creation him- or herself.   In *Bride of Frankie,* both the creator/god, and the creation/monster, are split into male/female pairs: the male Dr. Stein creates Monty, and his wife and assistant Frankie creates Shelley.

To understand the unique contribution of *Bride of Frankie,* we need to take a deeper look at the god-aspect of the creator, and unpack the idea of creation as a process. Because of the circumstances surrounding the writing of *Frankenstein* (1818/1831), Mary Shelley imbued her work with a metacommentary on creation. While the character of Victor Frankenstein created the creature, Mary Shelley created Victor Frankenstein.

> VICTOR WAS THE CHILD OF HER LITERARY WOMB. THE ONLY CHILD OF HERS SHE COULD ENSURE WOULD LIVE TO ADULTHOOD. AND YET STILL ONE THAT SHE COULD NOT, IN THE END, CONTROL.

Born of a mother who died shortly after childbirth, mother herself to miscarried and short-lived babies, Mary Shelley knew the sorrow of imperfect creation, uncontrollable creation, creation that could do nothing but cause death and instill sorrow in those around it. And having been raised in a non-religious, scientifically literate household, who was implicitly to blame for the death of her children and the death of her mother? She was.

It is without dispute that Mary Shelley blamed herself and her circumstances for the death of her children, and was well aware that her mother had died 11 days after giving birth to her. Mary Shelley wrote in a letter to a friend that she dreamed of resurrecting one of her babies after having found him dead, already cold, shortly after his birth. The threads of the tale of *Frankenstein* were taken from her life—from her desire to create and her understanding that when one sets oneself up, hubristically, as a creator, one cannot then control the life, death, or fate of the created being. It is, therefore, a form of self-fulfilling paradox that in the two hundred and few years since *Frankenstein* was published, the story's themes have persisted, but the reverence by the (screen) writers for the act of creation has not.

In story after story, the creations are *inherently* evil, destructive, violent, or bad, or at the very least, indifferent to human feelings or suffering. This has little to do with their exteriors—many of the creations are not grotesques, though they do remain uncanny—but their personalities are antithetical to co-existence with humans. Likewise, the creators are doing this for their own glorification.

This does bear similarity to Victor Frankenstein in Mary Shelley's original, however, Victor's realization of his mistaken actions, caused by hubris, are immediate—he becomes deathly ill as soon as the creation comes back to life—whereas, in the reimaginings, the consequences only come later, when the creature's inherently evil nature triumphs.

Yet the creature in Mary Shelley's novel is *not* evil. He is not good, either. He is human. Flawed, grotesque on the outside, and as un-learned as a newborn at first, he explores his surroundings, learns to walk, talk, clothe, and feed himself, and eventually, by covertly observing the world and humans around him, he learns about ethics and reasoning and the difference between good and evil. The mistakes he makes early on and the harm he does to himself and those around him reflect not an inhuman(e) evilness, but rather a very human fumbling—an imperfect ability to control a similarly imperfect physical, spiritual, and mental being. His actions later in the novel are evil, but they are not evil for evil's sake. He pursues revenge against a creator who abandoned him at birth, denounced his existence, would not endure his presence, and refused to make him a mate. It is no wonder he is angry, hurt, vengeful, and violent—his existence has been nothing but hatred and revulsion from the people he looked to for succor and solace.

But what if he had been cared for? What if Victor had claimed him, unrepentantly, explained the science of his creation to other scientists through learned publications, introduced the creation to his family, and created a female undead creation to be his partner? We see throughout analytical and theoretical writings that an absence of parental care can deeply impact behavior and development. What choices would the creation make if, instead of learning ethics and good from evil from other people, Victor had sat down with him and taught him? Would the creature have a long, happy, resurrected life then? *Bride of Frankie* answers this question.

THE NARRATIVE:
AN HOMAGE TO THE BEST AND MOST RIDICULOUS OF *FRANKENSTEIN* AND ITS DERIVATIVES

One of the staples of *Frankenstein*-based film is that while the creation might or might not live, the creator might and often does. We, the audience, are expected to be sympathetic to the creator—to the scientist whose "monster" escaped the lab. But in *Bride of Frankie,* Dr. Stein is different—he is difficult to root for or be sympathetic to. Snively gives her scientist every opportunity for redemption, but he is just… mean. Dr. Stein represents callousness, cruelty, and oppression to Frankie, Monty, and the homunculus. Redemption can only be had by those who actively seek it, and Dr. Stein is uninterested in such human feelings, whether in himself or anyone else. He dies unredeemed and unrepentant. These elements are there in Mary Shelley's original story, too, where Victor turns away from his family and his fiancée, and then cruelly oppresses his own creation, believing himself to be in the right, to the very end.

As the title suggests, although Frankie created Shelley for Monty, the creator and creation end up together. In contrast to the examples I have given of male characters, Shelley is both teachable and willing to try new things. As both Monty and Shelley start the film (un)dead, it would be easy to see the death narrative as centered around them. However, the denouement of the film involves the death of Dr. Stein and the re-death of Monty. When Monty dies defending the women against Dr. Stein, Frankie offers to re-resurrect him, but he demurs— he dies happily, having had friends, and having done good with his undeath. In this moment of genre-bending self-sacrifice, has Snively given us a new way to approach this particular type of death on the screen?

It would be easy to see all four characters (plus their mischievous homunculus, kept in a mason jar) as Jungian aspects of the masculine and feminine, but Snively does something much more subtle with her work. She challenges us to embrace the nurturing and caring elements within us all, and realize that kindness, attentiveness, and good behavior are taught, and thus can be learned by everyone. The film opens on a dark and stormy night. Our protagonist Frances (you can call her Frankie) pulls the iconic massive electrical switch, and her (female) creation shudders and groans, but then goes still. Frankie sighs and returns the switch to its original setting. But wait! The creation stirs and wakes. IT'S ALIVE! Frankie unplugs the creation (now Shelley), and we see a standard three-pronged socket in her neck.

In both Monty and Shelley, we also see that although the actors playing them are lovely people, there are touches of the grotesque in their presentations, which are not covered up or de-emphasized. Shelley has the standard Y incision of an autopsied corpse and a slash across her forehead, which she eventually pins closed with a safety pin (very grunge rock-esque). Monty has a row of stitches across his forehead and chest. And he is a very crude, unfinished person with rough manners, a tendency toward frustration, and a distinct lack of social and physical control. When interacting with Shelley, he tends to grapple, thrust, and express his id while Frankie patiently reprimands him.

At one point, Frankie exclaims, "Honestly, Monty, what's wrong with you!" and the scene changes to a flashback—Dr. Stein is heard in a voiceover saying, "You'll learn who's the master!" while shocking Monty with an electric prod. The torture, crudeness, lack of care and finesse, and the idea that might will triumph have influenced Monty's personality until he is someone who grabs a woman's breasts, fondles himself while she dances, and beats his own head against the wall and yells when frustrated. However, Frankie believes that Monty can be redeemed through patience, kindness, and friendship. She continues to draw the two creations together, reminding Monty to be gentle with Shelley, correcting his manners, and telling him that they must all be friends. No one deserves to be alone.

Here we hit the crux of the narrative—Frankie is alone in her relationship with Dr. Stein. Their wedding photo shows them standing apart, facing away from each other. Shortly after she revives Shelley, Frankie receives a telegram: *Collecting samples, gone another week, Victor.* And when he does come back, he categorically denies missing her, and she sees a lipstick mark on his shirt—he has been with someone else. When she confronts him, he deflects—"Don't go changing the subject; you had no right to mess with my work!" She replies, "'Your' work?! That's funny. I thought this was 'our' work!" He responds, "Clearly. I would never have made something so… repugnant." He nudges Monty and, looking over at Shelley, who is wearing a dress with a corset closure in the front, says, "Least she's got a nice rack, eh Monty?" Frankie slaps Dr. Stein, who slaps her back, sending her to the ground. Monty then slaps Dr. Stein, sending him to the ground as well. He lands near a fork discarded earlier and throws the fork at Monty, lodging it in Monty's exposed neck plug, causing a short circuit.

Monty ends up on the floor, twitching. Dr. Stein says, "You see what happens when you overstep your bounds, woman?" Frankie replies, "You're a monster!" The homunculus (who we find out in the end credits is named Tina) crashes a bookcase down on Dr. Stein, who chokes out, "Forgive me!" but Frankie's attention is only for Monty, who was also hit by the books. She cries out, "He's alive! Hang in there, Monty, I'm coming!" as she tries to find something to re-resurrect him. He stops her, saying, "No. Die now. Friends," and he dies again. The film ends with Shelley comforting Frankie and saying, "Friends, good." They move closer as they dance, and you know they will end up as much more than friends. There will be a Bride *for* Frankie.

THE UNLIMITED POTENTIAL OF RESURRECTION AS REBIRTH

In this short film, we see the unlimited potential of resurrection as rebirth and the expressiveness of the medium of film to explore it. There are three rebirths and one potential one in *Bride of Frankie*, the initial creation of Monty and Shelley, the possible second rebirth of Monty, which he refuses, and the rebirth of Frankie into a loved and fulfilled woman. Monty's first rebirth is the one we expect—he is Dr. Stein's monster, the analog to Mary Shelley's original creation. And he follows a similar narrative arc for a while. He is abused and discarded by his creator. His manners and expression are crude, having been truncated by the rejection and cruelty he endured.

Then, with the intercession of Frankie, things change—Monty learns about friendship, begins to be gentle and kind, and ultimately, he sacrifices himself for the women. Mary Shelley's monster does no such thing—the revulsion of everyone around him taints his second life, and, friendless, he pursues Victor Frankenstein to the ends of the earth, gleefully and sorrowfully watches his creator die, and then flees again into the arctic wilderness, where it is assumed he also eventually dies. Mary Shelley's creation's re-death is an inevitable consequence of his beleaguered life; having been created monstrous, and lived without love, he must die without redemption.

Monty's re-death, rather than being inevitable, is a choice he makes to preserve the lives of his friends. Monty sees the bookcase waver and holds Dr. Stein in place. When the bookcase comes crashing down on him and Dr. Stein, Monty understands that there is a way for the people he loves to live the lives they were meant for—Shelley and Frankie can have happiness through his sacrifice. Why die rather than continue to live, as Frankie is offering? While Frankie created Shelley *for* Monty, and he was making progress, he would have eternally been the third wheel. His narrative cycle was done. And in death, his story becomes beatific. The women will mourn him but move on with their lives.

This takes the form of dancing together at the end of the film. In it and several moments throughout, we see echoes of one of Dr. Stein's most stinging accusations. When he returns unexpectedly, Frankie says, "Dr. Stein! You're back early!" He replies, "To the contrary, Frankie, it looks like I'm too late. What have you done?!" She says, sadly, "I know, I should have waited. It's just… Monty was so depressed." And he comes back with, "Monty? Come now, Frankie, are you sure this wasn't about *you*?" Though he is boorish, violent, cruel, and domineering, he is also right in this instance. Everything about Shelley suits Frankie's tastes. She is easily taught, quickly picking up instruction in manners, dance, and speech. She defends herself against Monty's clumsy assaulting advances, but responds when he tries very hard to be better. She cares and has a heart. And when Shelley has difficulty with her silverware at the table, Frankie discovers: "Oh, of course! You're a leftie. Like… me." This third resurrection, that of Frankie as a loved woman who can freely love back, is the power of regeneration and the screen.

MARY SHELLEY'S ABSOLUTION, 200 YEARS IN THE MAKING

Through the creation of Shelley, unique among the *Frankenstein*-derived characters for her graceful, caring nature, and of Frankie, unique among the creators, Snively has given Mary Shelley a chance to be a mother of more than dead grotesques, mindless killers, or doomed hybrids. The derivatives, apart from the humor-genre ones, retain only the surface of *Frankenstein* and carry almost none of the subtext, focusing on the fact that the creator is playing god and not *why* the creator feels the need to play god. As Mary Shelley's *Frankenstein* (1818/1831) took on a life of its own (pun very much intended), we do not know if she forgave herself later in life. That miscarriages, stillbirths, childbed fever, and childhood deaths from unpreventable illness need no forgiveness is beside the point—Mary Shelley's premier novel was a beautiful self-flagellation for the "crime" of her failures as a mother. That her protagonist was male does not change this, for he is beset by women who do those things which Mary Shelley could not—nurture, protect, and sacrifice for their offspring—in the form of his own mother, and his intended bride, Elizabeth, and even the doomed Justine, framed for the crimes of Victor's own creation. Her creation, Victor, can only create imperfectly, can only birth dead things, can only fail to protect his family.

Frankie, however, does so much more. Frankie meets her creations where they are and works with them to achieve their true potentials.

> FRANKIE GIVES LIFE TO IMPERFECT CREATIONS, BUT DOES NOT DECRY THEIR IMPERFECTIONS—SHE ACCEPTS THEIR FLAWED, *HUMAN* CHARACTERISTICS, THEIR OWN INHERENT NATURES, AND HONES THEM TO BE GENTLER.

Frankie protects her family as much as she can and offers re-resurrection, a new chance, and rebirth. This makes all the difference, as shown in theoretical and practical writings on the topic of childhood behavior, and the creations, though in adult bodies, are in the learning phase of childhood.

What we can see in *Bride of Frankie* is an absolution of Mary Shelley, a re-writing of the narrative with the understanding that grotesques need love too, that the varying finalities of death can have beauty and grace, and that if given a choice, some creations die willingly, not merely from the fact that their creator did not try hard enough. It is, in effect, a celebration of the original text and an acknowledgment of Mary Shelley's metacommentary on creation.

Writing in a 2021 chapter about their work, Snively and Executive Producer Agustín Fuentes state:

> "Employing a casting agent in Chicago, we saw highly pedigreed actors straight from the prestigious Steppenwolf Theater, along with many boasting equally prestigious thespian credits. Yet, in attempting to play the role of 'a woman in a *Frankenstein* film,' the vast majority confined their interpretations to one of two stereotypes: a kindergarten teacher or a Mel Brooks' dominatrix.

> "Snively tried every last trick in her directing toolbox, and yet most could not get past these preconceived notions of 'the female' in Frankenstein. The one woman who came in, and without any direction whatsoever, performed the role perfectly, unabashedly in a Shelleyian note, was a woman who had not seen a single one of the film adaptations but had read Shelley's novel."

It took the radical act of finding someone with no knowledge of the screen-based derivatives of *Frankenstein* to bring a kind, caring creator to the screen, and to allow the male creation to have a good death, and the female creation to have a long, happy life.

References:

Alien 3, David Fincher (Director), 20th Century Fox, 1992.

Alita: Battle Angel, Robert Rodriguez (Director), 20th Century Fox, 2019.

Black Mirror: Be Right Back (Season 2, Episode 1), Owen Harris (Director), Zeppotron, 2013.

Blade Runner, Ridley Scott (Director), Warner Bros., 1982.

Blade Runner 2049, Denis Villeneuve (Director), Alcon Entertainment, 2017.

Bride of Frankie, Devi Snively (Director), Deviant Pictures, 2017.

Clueless, Amy Heckerling (Director), Paramount Pictures, 1995.

Doyle, Sady, *Dead Blondes and Bad Mothers: Monstrosity, Patriarchy, and the Fear of Female Power,* New York, NY: Penguin Random House, 2019.

Ex Machina, Frank Garland, Universal Pictures, 2014.

Faber, Liz, *When Robots Choose to Die: A Survey of Robot Suicide in Science Fiction*, Washington, DC: PCA/ACA National Conference, 2019.

Frankenhooker, Frank Henenlotter (Director), Levins-Henenlotter, 1990.

Frankenstein, James Whale (Director), Universal Pictures, 1931.

Frankenweenie, Tim Burton (Director), Walt Disney Pictures, 2012.

Goodenough, Ward, *Description and Comparison in Cultural Anthropology,* Piscataway, NJ: Aldine Transaction, 1970.

Lucy, Luc Besson (Director), Europa Corp, 2014.

Montillo, Rosanne, *The Lady and Her Monsters: A Tale of Dissections, Real-Life Dr. Frankensteins, and the Creation of Mary Shelley's Masterpiece*, New York, NY: Harper Collins, 2013.

My Fair Lady, George Cukor (Director), Warner Bros., 1964.

Pan's Labyrinth, Guillermo del Toro (Director), Estudio Picasso, 2006.

Pryor, Campbell, Amy Perfors, and Piers Howe, Even Arbitrary Norms Influence Moral Decision Making, in *Nature Human Behavior*, 2018.

Re-Animator, Stuart Gordon (Director), Empire Pictures, 1985.

RoboCop, Paul Verhoeven (Director), Orion Pictures, 1987.

Shelley, Mary Wollstonecraft. 1818/1831. Frankenstein; or, The Modern Prometheus. London: Lackington, Hughes, Harding, Mavor, & Jones.

Snively, Devi, and Fuentes, Agustín. 2021. Masculinity, and Not Femininity, as Gendered 'Nature' in Cinematic Adaptations of Mary Shelley's *Frankenstein*, in *Gender, Supernatural Beings, and the Liminality of Death: Monstrous Males/Fatal Females,* Rebecca Gibson and James M. VanderVeen, eds., pgs. 135-147.

Splice, Vincenzo Natali (Director), Canal+, 2009.

Star Trek: The Next Generation: Datalore (Season 1, Episode 12), Rob Bowman (Director), Paramount Television, 1988.

Star Wars, George Lucas (Director), Lucasfilm, 1977.

The Bride of Frankenstein, James Whale (Director), Universal Pictures, 1935.

The Fly, David Cronenberg (Director), SLM Production Group, 1986.

The Maker, Christopher Kezelos (Director), Zealous Creative, 2012.

The Rocky Horror Picture Show, Jim Sharman (Director), 20th Century Fox, 1975.

The Skin I Live In, Pedro Almodóvar (Director), Blue Haze Entertainment, 2011.

The Spirit of the Beehive, Victor Erice (Director), Elías Querejeta Producciones Cinematográficas S.L., 1973.

We Need To Talk About Kevin, Lynne Ramsay (Director), BBC Films, 2011.

Young Frankenstein, Mel Brooks (Director), Gruskoff/Venture Films, 1974.

Werewolf for God: The Turbulent Trial of Thiess of Kaltenbrunn

Sarah Blake

Of all the monsters created throughout our history, there is a special kind of terror invoked by werewolves. Brutal and bloodthirsty, these creatures are depicted as walking among us, a sort of lycan Jekyll and Hyde, until they are brought out by the powers of the full moon, transforming an everyday person into an uncontrollable beast with otherworldly strength and a craving for flesh.

While they appear today as pure fiction in film, television, and art, there was a time when much of Europe considered these human-wolf hybrids to be a genuine threat, leaving horrifying trails of chaos in their paths.

The accounts from the European werewolf trials in the 1500-1600s are soaked in gore, with Peter Stubbe, Michel Verdun, Pierre Bourgot, Philibert Montot, Gilles Garnier, and the family of Folkert Dirks being only some of the

Pen and ink drawing dated 1580 of a werewolf terrorizing a town by Johann Jakub Wick.

names written in blood. These people were tortured, tried, and confessed to gruesome crimes all over Europe, claiming that they would transform into wolves before hunting children and livestock, tearing them limb from limb, and devouring them in violent rampages.

The church became obsessed with finding and killing these unholy beings, believing that these people were in league with Satan and entirely responsible for the atrocities they committed. Almost anything could tie someone to being a werewolf and doom them to a merciless end, even living near wolves or a person seeing a wolf that "looked like" someone. With all the paranoia, bloodshed, and extreme nature of the trials, it's difficult to imagine how one case could stand out from the rest.

But then there is Thiess of Kaltenbrunn.

On April 28, 1691, a Livonian farmhand named Thiess was brought into a courtroom in Jürgensburg, Swedish Livonia (present-day southern Estonia and northern Latvia.). A man in his 80s, he was in court for a fairly mundane reason, to serve as a witness in a trial against a suspected church thief. Upon taking the oath of witnesses, an innkeeper from Kaltenbrunn smirked when he saw his tenant, Thiess, taking the same oath. When asked why this made him smile, the innkeeper explained that it was amusing to see an oath be taken by Thiess, a man who was a known werewolf who ran with the Devil. For most people, this was a severe accusation they would only admit to after being severely tortured. But Thiess's reaction was amazingly calm. He confirmed that yes, he was once a werewolf, but he gave it up a decade ago. Why did this matter, though? After all, he was a werewolf for God.

Standing before the stunned judges, Thiess expanded on his unusual claim. Every year he and his fellow werewolves carried out their duty of visiting Hell to battle Satan and ensure a good upcoming harvest. This mission occurred three times throughout the year, on Pentecost Eve, St. John's Eve, and St. Lucia's Eve before Christmas. But, he clarified that sometimes, the first two dates were slightly different based on how the grain was blooming.

When the judges pressed him for details, Thiess easily obliged. He explained that sorcerers roamed the land every year, snatching up as much grain, livestock, and produce as possible, bringing it down to

Hell to serve the Devil who rewarded them. On the three appointed days, Thiess and the other werewolves gathered together and donned a pelt that turned them into wolves. This pelt was given to him by a peasant years ago, but he would not name them. Once transformed, the wolves traveled by foot to the "end of the lake called Puer Esser, in a swamp below Lemburg about a half-mile from Klingenberg." No one ever saw them enter. "It's not on top but under the earth," he explained, "and the entrance is protected by a gate that no one can find, except someone who belongs inside."

Throughout his testimony, Thiess explained that their arrival to Hell was never welcomed, and the task required some planning:

> *"There were lordly chambers and commissioned doorkeepers, who stoutly resist those who want to take back the grain blossoms and the grain the sorcerers brought there. The grain blossoms were guarded in a special container and the grain in another."* He went on to explain that there were also *hellhounds in Hell, but there was nothing for werewolves to worry about, they "could easily escape the dogs and the guards might well have shot at them, if they could get near them. The hellhounds did nothing to them."*

If the mission was a success, there was reason to celebrate. Once the werewolves claimed back everything that the sorcerers took from the land, they would return to the surface and throw everything into the air, returning prosperity to everyone.

It's hard to imagine the atmosphere in the courtroom. Here was a man who fully and absolutely told them that he was a werewolf, a bloodthirsty creature that was tearing people apart and eating children all over Europe. How was it possible that he was a werewolf, but instead of being a monster, one that served God and ensured successful harvests and good health for his countrymen?

German woodcut depicting a werewolf, dated 1722.

There were obviously many, many questions for Thiess, and they started with some basics. He claimed that the group of werewolves, which could number up to 30, would feed on only small animals that they roasted and ate together. The court asked how they got the fire and tools to do so, and Thiess gave them the obvious answer, they took equipment from a farm and used it to cook the food. Nothing was eaten raw—they were not savages after all. When asked if he took part in these meals, he responded with, "Yes, and so what?" Why did they not eat the meat raw if they were wolves? The answer was again amazingly matter-of-fact: "That wasn't the way. Rather, they eat it like men, roasted." How did they do all of this if they had wolf heads and paws? How could they handle the tools needed to cook? Once again, Thiess stated what seemed so obvious to him, they used their teeth and cooked the meat on spits, and, he reminded them again, when they ate the food, they were men, not wolves.

These questions scratched the surface, but there was a grave issue at hand here. This man was a werewolf, a creature associated with Satan himself, which was enough to warrant his torture and execution. But, when pressed about his connections to Satan, Thiess was adamant that he was on their side, working *against* the Devil for the benefit of all. When asked if the Devil ate with them, he firmly denied it, stating that only the evil sorcerers ate with the Devil in Hell; the Devil can't stand the werewolves because they take back what the sorcerers stole for him. Thiess pointed out the importance of their mission and their timing to the court:

"In the previous year, he and the others had delayed, and they did not come into hell at the right time when the gates were still open, so they couldn't carry off the grain blossoms and the grain the sorcerers had taken inside, and we had a bad year for grain. But this year, he and the others did the right things at the proper time. The witness himself brought out of hell as much barley, oats, and rye as he could carry. Therefore, this year we have all kinds of grain in abundance, although more oats than barley."

At this point in the testimony, things took an even more serious turn. When asked where werewolves go after death, Thiess replied, "They are buried like other people, and their souls come to heaven, but the Devil takes the sorcerers' souls for himself." He was asked if he listens faithfully to the word of God, prays diligently, and if he takes the Lord's Supper. He said no. The court then asked him how it was possible that a man who does not go to church, pray, or take the Lord's Supper can go to God. According to the court transcript, the response from Thiess was scathing:

"The werewolves do not serve the Devil, for they take away from him that which the sorcerers brought him, and for that reason, the Devil is so hostile to them that he cannot bear them. Rather, he has them driven off with iron goads, as if they were dogs, for the werewolves are God's hounds. But the sorcerers serve the Devil and do everything according to his will, therefore, their souls belong to him. Everything the werewolves do profits people best, for if they didn't exist and the devil made off with the

prosperity, robbed or stole it, all the world's prosperity would depart..."

Thiess continued, asking, "Why should God not accept his soul, even if he didn't go to church or take the Lord's Supper, for in his youth he was not properly instructed in this."

Whatever fascination may have allowed Thiess to tell his story for this long was gone. From what the court was hearing, this man was a werewolf associated with the Devil and that should have been enough, but he now fully admitted that he did not attend church, did not pray, and did not participate in the Lord's Supper. This was not acceptable.

By turning into a wolf, denying his human form, and killing livestock, the court accused Thiess of breaking his contract with God, but he fired back that most people did much worse. Also, he stated he did pray a small amount, the few things taught to him by the pastor he worked for, but that was it. He was simply too old to learn anything new. It was here that Thiess admitted that, based on other court cases, he should have ended him. He previously stated he had not been a werewolf in a decade, but that was a lie. He was still a werewolf because the only way for him to

17th-18th Century woodcut depicting a human-wolf hybrid.

remove it from himself was to pass it along to someone else who would willingly and knowingly take up the mantle.

The court demanded what benefits he had being a werewolf. He told them none. They asked if he wanted to die a werewolf. He said no.

When asked if he intended to turn back to God before his death, Thiess first did not answer, stating who knows where his soul would go. The hearing could have ended multiple times, but the courtroom was far from done with Thiess, and he was far from done with them.

Now that Thiess's sins of being a werewolf were established, the court wanted to address a well-known rumor that he knew how to tell the future, and they demanded to know where he got this ability. This gift of prophecy was something the old man denied. He did not know the future—he was just a farmhand who tended to the medical needs of the horses. He could have stopped there, but Thiess went ahead and told them that his means of helping the horses was through different incantations used to remove the evils put upon them by the Devil. It wasn't just horses either. Thiess used several different words, herbs, charms, and methods to heal sick and wounded people, sometimes receiving money or livestock in return. The court asked if he could harm someone with his methods. He answered that no, everything he did was done for the good. But, he added, "Whoever did evil to him, things would not go well for him."

When the pastor was brought in, the courtroom grew fiery. Herr Pastor laid into Thiess, asking him why he chose to go against his commitment to God and assuring him that if he sincerely repented, he would be forgiven and shown great mercy. The old self-proclaimed werewolf had had enough, and according to the court transcript:

> ...he showed himself truly obstinate and remained insistent that all he had done was no sin against God. Rather, he had done God much service thereby in fulfillment of His will that they recover the prosperity from the Devil, which the sorcerers had carried to him, and he thereby did good for the whole land. They also shared the prosperity with one another, and this year would turn out well... The sorcerers were God's enemies and had no portion in heaven, but they (i.e., the werewolves) were God's friends and hunting dogs, whom he uses against the

Devil and the sorcerers, and therefore their souls
came to heaven.

The pastor and Thiess went back and forth, with one side urging to ask forgiveness and the other vehemently saying there was nothing to be forgiven for. Thiess insisted that nothing he did was evil and then told the pastor that he was too young to understand what was being said to him. After all, said Thiess, if what he was doing with his herbs and charms was so evil, why were others who practiced the same methods not being tried and accused of working for Satan? It was not fair, and he would not stand for it. The verbal tug of war continued until, finally, the accused could take no more. He finally gave in and said he would give it all up—he was too old and feeble to continue on both in his werewolfism and in this testimony.

At this point, the focus was supposed to turn back to the original purpose of this entire hearing, the church thief Pirsen Tönnis. But, how could they possibly focus on something like theft when they were in the presence of one of "God's hounds?" The questioning of Tönnis and a local peasant named Gurrian quickly turned back to the subject of Thiess, with the two discussing how the old man used charms, incantations to the sun and moon, and salt that he consecrated himself to bring people health, blessings, and prosperity. At first, Gurrian denied any involvement with Thiess, but eventually, he came clean, "adding the reason he had lied and that it really meant nothing, also that nothing evil or wicked had been done. Who wouldn't want to have prosperity for the grain and help and advice regarding a sick animal?"

As Thiess was escorted out of the courtroom that day, all present were left with a serious and extremely confusing case on their hands. Over the course of his testimony, the old man had seemingly damned himself repeatedly. He admitted freely to being a werewolf and engaging on a regular basis with Satan and his sorcerers. He did not pray or take part in worshiping God. He was well versed in using charms, herbs, and incantations to the sun and moon to manifest outcomes for himself and others. He angrily defied a pastor, telling him he did not know what he was talking about. He stated plainly that for anyone who committed evil against him, "things would not go well for him." On paper, this painted the portrait of an extremely dangerous man that should be removed from existence immediately. But what if he was telling the truth? What if it *was* him ensuring successful harvests for all of his countrymen?

> WAS THERE SIN IN HEALING THE SICK AND GRANTING PROSPERITY? COULD THE GUISE OF EVIL BE MASKING TRUE GOODNESS?

After many months the verdict was finally in. The list of offenses by Thiess was long and extremely frightening, but somehow, miraculously, his life was spared. The charmer, farmer, and werewolf for God was sentenced to a public flogging of 20 blows and "banishment from the land forever."

After his turbulent trial, Thiess disappeared not only from his land but seemingly from all historical records, and his fate remains unknown. The werewolf trials of Europe raged on, extending into the 18th Century before finally fading out alongside the much more well-known witch trials of the same era. Amazingly, the transcript of this trial was lost until it was rediscovered in the 1920s, giving legal history a new and incredible story.

Could a werewolf be good? Based on the judgment, the court seems to have entertained the notion that it was possible. The werewolf trial of Thiess is a chapter of history that stands alone. At a time of absolute terror, fanaticism, and turmoil, one accused man admitted to actions that typically ensured certain death, threw a wrench into the system, and challenged the courtroom with questions of what truly constituted good or evil.

There's the wolf in sheep's clothing, and then there is the man called Thiess.

References:
Old Thiess, a Livonian Werewolf A Classic Case in Comparative Perspective
by Carlo Ginzburg and Bruce Lincoln.
press.uchicago.edu/sites/thiess/old_thiess_transcript.pdf

POOR, MAD HUMANITY

Stacey Ryall

Upon roaming the halls of Ararat's sprawling, abandoned "lunatic" asylum for the first time, I captioned a subsequent social media post with the words "I belong here." It was simply a quip, but the reality is that—not too long ago—women were considered to belong in these very asylums for ailments that are both prevalent and treatable in our current society.

> LITTLE DID I KNOW THAT SOON ENOUGH I'D SUFFER A FATE THAT MADE ME FEEL, WITHOUT A DOUBT, THAT THE ONLY PLACE FOR ME WAS AN ASYLUM.

Like many of us, I grew up watching paranormal television, which only intensified my interest in the unknown. I was an insomniac as a child, convinced my bedroom in the suburbs of Melbourne, Australia, was filled with ghosts, and every ceiling creak was an evil spirit ready to attack me in my sleep. In hindsight, I don't believe my bedroom was "filled with ghosts," I simply had an overactive imagination and read too many *Goosebumps* books. Then, with the help of American television, my interest in the macabre changed from terror to intrigue. When I traveled to the United States in both 2011 and 2016—in addition to the usual tourist hotspots—I was determined to visit the eerie locations I'd only experienced through the box. When

I returned, I realized I had neglected the history, aura, and mythology of my own backyard. I had explored Philadelphia's Eastern State Penitentiary, taken a New Orleans ghost tour, and meandered through Hollywood Forever Cemetery before even considering the strange locales available in my home state of Victoria. I eventually discovered a tantalizing history of the early days of mental health treatment and locations that to this day remain intact—and accessible—to the curious public.

The discovery of gold in Victoria in 1851 triggered a local gold rush, and a dramatic population expansion followed. Among the many challenges the authorities faced was the neglected area of mental health. Originally, people suffering from mental illness were detained in the city jail. This was obviously inadequate, and the growing population also made it impossible. Crime was high in the young city of Melbourne, and the jail facilities overflowed.

Yarra Bend, an area north of the city, was selected for a mental hospital—an enclave of land further up the city's famous Yarra River. The original buildings set on 620 acres were modest, built out of bluestone, with seven cells and two wards for men, and three cells and one ward for women.

Yarra Bend Asylum cottages, c. 1858-1864. Photographed by Jean Baptiste Charlier.

Admission was initially at the Governor's prudence—prospective inmates had to be certified as "mentally unsound" by a medical professional, and then have their transfer to the hospital approved by the Governor himself. But once the asylum was in operation, and the number of inmates began to grow, this procedure was abandoned.

In 1852, reports of atypical care and patient abuse surfaced within the asylum. An inquiry was held, and lurid testimony was supplied. Among the charges: physical and sexual abuse of patients, dirty and unhygienic

The new Kew Asylum, overlooking the original Yarra Bend Asylum, c. 1870-1880. Photographer unknown.

facilities, and corruption. By 1870, the asylum had swollen to more than 1,000 inmates. Again, facing overcrowding and reports of inhumane conditions, the State Government began to consider a substitute. A new mental hospital in the suburb of Kew was proposed, and the Kew Asylum opened in 1871. Around this time, new institutions were also opened in rural Victoria—Ararat and Beechworth.

The Government of Victoria originally envisioned that Yarra Bend would be closed once Kew, Ararat, and Beechworth asylums were established. However, a further population explosion in the colony increased the burden on the new asylums. This was compounded by the historic practice of housing "inebriates," "idiots," and "imbeciles" at lunatic asylums.

Yarra Bend eventually stopped accepting patients in 1925. The remaining patients were relocated to other facilities. Inspector General for the Insane, Dr. Ernest Jones, provided a gloomy epitaph for the place he helped to close:

> *The airing courts were very small and damnable, with high bluestone walls preventing all view of the surrounding countryside. There was also a row of outside cells, with earth closets, two dark padded cells, and an all-pervading smell of poor, mad humanity.*

The asylum was severely damaged by a fire in 1982 and was mostly demolished as a result. There is very little evidence left of the facility's existence. A lone pillar from the old entrance gate, alongside a small information board, is all that remains. Some of the brick foundation walls of the asylum still exist below ground level.

Kew Lunatic Asylum, c. 1885-1887. Photograph by Charles Nettleton.

The Kew Asylum was closed in 1988, and the main building and grounds have since been converted into apartments. There are, however, structures remaining outside of the city that are open for public exploration, and the opportunity to gain a greater understanding of the history of the Victorian mental health system.

North of the state, towards the New South Wales border, is Beechworth—a town with a rich gold mining history and a main street that remains historically accurate and quaint. Overlooking the town from a nearby hill is the decommissioned Mayday Hills Lunatic Asylum, which at its peak of operation consisted of 67 buildings and was home to over 1,200 patients and 500 staff. A list of reasons for admission to Mayday for the period of 1867-1910 included grief, nerves, hysteria, depression, overwork… and general "Women's Afflictions."

Beechworth Lunatic Asylum, 1866. Photograph by Algernon Hall.

The hospital closed in 1998 after 128 years of operation. Few of those buildings remain, but enough relics linger as a reminder of the scale and history of the institute. The few that remain are also rich in hauntings, so says our ghost tour guide, who escorted us through the deserted buildings and shared a multitude of titillating stories and myths.

On two occasions, I have toured the asylum, and on two occasions, I have been touched by unseen hands—in one instance, a playful entity enjoyed twirling my mother's hair through its "hands" in the dark. It's a distressing thought that some patients may remain imprisoned even in the afterlife but also pause for contemplation that perhaps what remains is simply the energy of an emotionally-charged facility. One where lives were suspended, confined, and sometimes ended. More than a morbid fascination, for me, there was something more than a curiosity about the ability to explore these facilities—a compassion, a connection. The introductory quote from 19th Century alienist Dr. John Conolly in Jill Guise's *The Maddest Place on Earth* may explain it:

> "EVERY MAN IS INTERESTED IN THIS SUBJECT; FOR NO MAN CAN CONFIDENTLY RECKON ON THE CONTINUANCE OF HIS PERFECT REASON."

I chose Beechworth as the first getaway I took with my boyfriend, Josh. He was interested in history, which was enough for me to assume he would humor me and my unique ghost hunting pastime. In the short time that we had been together, I got the feeling he was able to accept me and my peculiarities unconditionally. We stayed in Mayday Hills' old nurses' quarters, which have been converted into a quaint Art Deco accommodation. As you ponder the night's events, mere steps from the spirits you've just connected with, the old lodging creaks and moans throughout the night as you drift away, dreaming into another time.

Mayday Hills has mercifully been declared "architecturally significant" by Heritage Victoria as an "exceptionally fine example of a widespread complex of Italianate-style asylum buildings dating from the 1860s, and in the case of the surrounding cottages, the 1880s." All three of the major Victorian asylums are built in a similar style.

A morning wander through the grounds, searching out the remains of the "ha-ha wall," gave us time to reflect on the facility's significance by daylight. This retaining wall was built to prevent patients from escaping, constructed to appear low from the inside thanks to a trench formed on the inside, but too high to climb over. The unusual name is thought to refer to either its half up/half down appearance, or—more cruelly—the practice of laughing at those on the inside.

Beechworth Lunatic Asylum, c. 1900-1909. Artist unknown.

The equally impressive Aradale Lunatic Asylum in Ararat was established in 1867. It consisted of 65 buildings sitting on five acres, so large it was at one stage a fully self-supporting city within a city. Construction began in 1866 and was opened for patients in 1867. Over almost 130 years, the asylum housed thousands of patients ranging from the criminally insane to those with mental illness and other conditions.

Among Aradale's carefully curated ghost tour are stories of bizarre history, brutal treatments, and (of course) masses of ghost stories. Traveling through the administration building, chapel, kitchen, surgery theatres, morgue, and the cavernous cell blocks, time truly stands still. Reported supernatural encounters include tickling, strange smells, banging sounds, shadows, and other unnerving sensations. Aradale was closed as an asylum in 1993. At its height, it provided a secure treatment facility housing over 1,000 patients.

FRONT VIEW OF THE LUNATIC ASYLUM

Front view of the Ararat Lunatic Asylum, c. 1877-1883. Photographer unknown.

I was planning on dragging Josh to see Aradale at some point, but in 2020 he tragically and unexpectedly passed away. We were just beginning our life together and planning an exciting future. I had found my person. And I suspect, despite my eccentricities, he had found his. Amidst the general fogginess of grief, I also experienced bouts of physical hysteria, depression, and intense nervousness. I thought back to my time exploring lunatic asylums and the compassion I felt for these poor, "mad" souls—particularly the women—whom our community did not yet have the proper tools to support.

"I belong here," indeed.

Maybe we all did at one point or another. Thankfully, we now have the support systems in place to avoid a padded cell and other objectionable methodologies. Moreover, we all should be able to find compassion for those in our history (and at present) who were not so fortunate.

References:

The Museum of Lost Things (https://www.museumoflost.com/the-lost-cemetery/)

Palace of Broken Dreams: A Brief History of Beechworth Asylum (2017, Asylum Ghost Tours)

The Maddest Place on Earth – Jill Giese (2018, Australian Scholarly Publishing Pty Ltd)

All royalty-free images are courtesy of State Library of Victoria

THE DARKEST HUE

Jillian Walkowiak

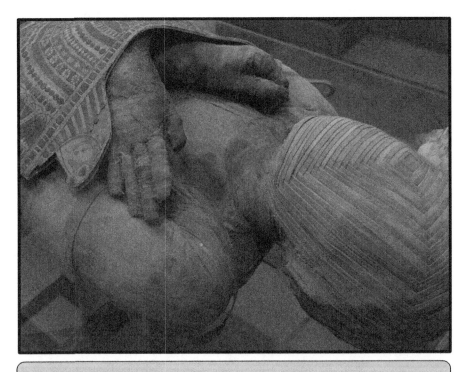

Egyptian mummy
Photo courtesy of priscillaip/CC BY-SA 2.0

Since the housing market in 2022 is abysmal, many homeowners have taken to sprucing up their current abodes instead of wading into the greed-infested waters of modern homebuying. It's always fun to head to the local hardware or home décor shop, poring through paint swatches to find the perfect shade or selecting the perfect art piece to make your old home feel new again. But how would you feel if, unbeknownst to you, that new, luxurious item was made up of things long dead?

Many of us choose to fill our homes with remnants of the deceased. We keep the ashes of beloved relatives in decorative containers on shelves. Taxidermized trophies are kept in ways as varied as wall hangings or wearable accessories. With all of this, there is a level of respect, as there is in most cultures' ways of treating their deceased.

Desecration of corpses is a widespread societal taboo. However, if that body has been around for a while—say 2,000 years or so—it seems all bets are off. The use of ground-up, ancient Egyptian mummies as an artist's pigment, is a perfect example of this alternate treatment of a corpse.

Mummy brown, or *caput mortum*, was a rich brown paint, a shade in between burnt umber and raw umber (you remember those Crayolas in the big box) made from the "fleshiest parts" of ancient mummies (no crayon reference for that). This lacquer supposedly had good transparency and could be used as either oil paint or as a watercolor pigment. Its use came to prominence in Europe in the late 1700s and 1800s. Some of the artists that were reported to use this horrific hue were Eugene Delacroix, Sir William Beechley, Angelica Kaufman, and Sir Lawrence Alma-Tadema. It is not known how aware they all were of what their artistic mediums contained, but some wholeheartedly embraced the practice.

Musician Among Children *by Martin Drölling.* Photo courtesy of the National Museum of Warsaw

There was a French artist named Martin Drölling who lived from 1752 to 1817. He was primarily known for painting general interest-type subjects, such as home interiors and individual portraits. His medium, however, was anything but ordinary as it is rumored that Drölling used his own version of mummy brown that was made with the bodies of exhumed French kings, taken from an abbey in Paris. The corpse trade was rampant in those days, and the French were none too pleased with their ruling class for a large portion of Drölling's life, so one can only imagine how he got his hands on those royal remains.

Artists were not the only ones involved in this grisly pursuit. Parts of ancient Egyptian mummified remains had been widely used since the 1200s in everything from art to delicacies to medicine. There was an 18th Century novelty shop called "*Á la Momie*" in France that sold "powdered mummies, incense, and myrrh."

POETS AND STORYTELLERS EXTOLLED THE VIRTUES OF THESE BIZARRE USES OF THE DECEASED, STATING THAT IT ALLOWED THOSE NO LONGER WITH US TO LIVE FOR ETERNITY THROUGH SUCH VARIED METHODS.

A noble idea, but based on how the ancient Egyptians viewed death and the dead, it's not certain that this was what they had in mind.

When an ancient Egyptian died, it was thought that the soul stayed in the body as it was used to and comfortable with this life on earth. Special priests followed detailed guidelines on embalming all corpses, from the most elite to the poorest of society, with modified options available for different classes. While this preservation process took up to 70 days, it was just the first step in death's journey, with the final destination being eternal joy in the Field of Reeds. The wealthy and the royal got massive, multi-roomed tombs as waystations, each filled with everything the traveler might need in the afterlife, from gold to food to beloved, mummified pets. The rest of society was typically buried in deep pits in the sand, taking a bit less with them. As an interesting quirk of nature, due to the naturally dry climate of Northern Africa, all these bodies were naturally mummified in similar ways and easily recognizable to pillagers hundreds of years later. All the care and precision were wasted as these ancient tombs were eventually ransacked.

An account given by a merchant from London describes one of his 16th Century visits to an ancient tomb. He was lowered into the grave by ropes and made his way through by candlelight. Upon reaching the room containing the actual bodies, it became a free-for-all. Bodies were destroyed. Corpses were torn asunder, with limbs being broken off and examined. The merchant goes on to state that not only did he bring home 600 pounds of remains for his employer but that he also kept "one little hand I brought into England, to shew [show]; and presented it to my brother." One can guess that a portion of those pounds of desiccated flesh inevitably became the infamous *caput mortum* paint.

As with most fads, the use of mummy brown eventually went out of vogue. The discovery of the Rosetta Stone in 1799 led to a clearer understanding of ancient Egyptian society, recognizing its vast historical significance. Unfortunately, by this point, many tombs had been looted and hundreds of bodies destroyed. But as a small silver lining, the dwindling supply of mummies, as well as Europeans' changing attitudes, mummy brown paint would slowly go out of common circulation. Its use was derided as barbaric by artists and critics alike. When some painters became fully aware of what was actually on their palettes, they reacted quite strongly.

It is said that when the British artist Edward Burne-Jones, born in 1833, discovered that he was painting with corpses, he was horrified. He took his well-used tube of

Portrait of Caroline Fitzgerald by Edward Burne-Jones, painted 1884.
Photo courtesy of University of Toronto

mummy brown out to his back garden and gave it a proper burial, complete with a ceremony and flowers to mark the spot. Burne-Jones himself died in 1898, and while he was finished with such creepy colors, it would continue to exist in the shadows for 66 more years.

The UK paint manufacturer that commercially produced mummy brown was C. Roberson & Co., which opened in 1810 and is still in existence today. In 1964, the company regrettably informed the public that their obscure and morbid paint was officially discontinued as they had essentially run out of mummies.

> THEY WENT ON TO STATE, "WE MIGHT HAVE A FEW ODD LIMBS LYING AROUND SOMEWHERE, BUT NOT ENOUGH TO MAKE ANY MORE PAINT."

So when your home has been freshly redone, and that newly acquired painting—maybe picked up at a garage sale or gallery—is situated in a lovely spot in your living room, don't be surprised if you feel an unusual presence. There is a chance that a part of someone from centuries past is contained in that canvas, and they are probably not very happy about it.

References:

Mark, Joshua J. "Egyptian Afterlife – The Field of Reeds". 28 March 2016. *World History Encyclopedia.* https://www.worldhistory.org/article/877/egyptian-afterlife---the-field-of-reeds/ Accessed 30 May 2022.

Mccouat, Phillip. "The Life and Death of Mummy Brown". *Journal of Art in Society*. 2013. https://www.artinsociety.com/the-life-and-death-of-mummy-brown.html. Accessed 30 May 2022.

Torres, R. Leopoldina. "A Pigment from the Depths". *Harvard Art Museums*. 31 October, 2013. https://harvardartmuseums.org/article/a-pigment-from-the-depths. Accessed 30 May 2022.

THE ~~SWORD~~ SPIRIT IN THE STONE

Tiffiny Rose Allen

Most of us have heard or are at least familiar with the story of *The Sword in the Stone*—only someone true of heart can remove it from the sedimentary that is holding it. One thing I have learned when it comes to stones, regardless of whether they are sedimentary or crystal, is that sometimes they contain spirits of their own.

There are stories of the super seven crystal (mostly known as a variant of the amethyst crystal), containing multiple other minerals, separating it from the traditional stone we all know and becoming its own. I have heard that some people say each individual piece possesses its own spirit, its own energy, whispering and guiding us where to go.

The super seven stone is also known as Melody's stone or the sacred seven. It is only found in a region in Brazil named *Espirito Santo*, which translates to Holy Spirit. The minerals contained within the super seven crystal are amethyst, cacoxenite, goethite, lepidocrocite, rutile, smokey quartz, and clear quartz.

There are a number of stones that are considered to be tools, vessels, or channelers for angelic or divine energy. Granted, since stones come from the earth and carry their own vibrations, they all must contain some bout of divine essence (in my opinion, at least). Still, it comes down to what precisely you're trying to tap into and the difference in the energy of the stones or crystals you choose to work with.

For example, some people believe that the crystal known as moldavite, which is found in Moldova (hence the name), holds extraterrestrial energy or even spirit forms, as it came from a meteor that crashed to earth. The energies within such a stone are sure to be out of this world, but how can we know if it actually contains such an entity?

Some people like to sit with their crystals and feel them in their hands, therefore connecting to the stone's energy, inviting it into one's aura space, and tuning

Photo courtesy of Onohej Zlatove

into the frequency. It can be a debatable matter, but I like to think that some spirits reveal themselves only to those they desire to… I mean, wouldn't you?

One thing I have noticed about super seven and moldavite is that they contain a large number of energetic waves.

I can't say whether any spirits have visited me through the stones, but I know there is something there. The first time I ever held a piece of moldavite, I got a raging headache, and when I started working with super seven, I felt like I was floating. These are only two of a few stones I can account for, but I know that something about them is definitely otherworldly.

A sword can forge courage, strength, and honor by being released from a stone, but how can the stone tell that the person who now wields this blade is worthy? Perhaps there is a spirit channeling itself through the grit, sediment, and crystal structures? Maybe even it is your own wisdom and intuition guiding the energies?

Whatever the cause, I will always be amazed by how I have connected to stones and crystals and how they have somehow become friends of mine.

A Brief Guide to Working with Any Crystal:

• **Get to know your crystal.** Sit and hold it in your hand or lay down and place it on your chest. See if you can tap into the energy it provides.

• **Carry your crystal with you.** See if there is any difference in the energies or people surrounding you. Do you feel any different? Do your surroundings feel different?

• **Work with your crystal daily**, keep up a routine for a week or a month, and see if there is any difference from your past and present self.

• **Journal about your experience** and about the crystal you chose. What is it known to aid? What do you feel when you gaze upon it?

THE DIGITAL WEIRD

Amy L Bennett

I have a birthday this year. You probably do as well, but I can only ponder my own existence as a human for nearly 39 years because I have no idea how old you might be. At this age, though, something strange has begun to happen. I'm old enough to reflect on almost two decades of my attempts to experience and interact with the unknown and how I've done so with others in the same field.

In that time, there has been a lot of fluidity in what is considered popular ideology, role models, theories recycled and renewed again, what constitutes different parts of the paranormal at large and how it is interacted with. The paranormal on social platforms encompasses a significant portion of how society shares and interacts with this content, and I say this in the context of the Strange and Unusual because I've noticed something: I have been a woman, voluntarily including myself in paranormal social media for over a decade now. The growth and constant barrage of curated and algorithmically driven content can alter how we interpret unexplainable phenomena and how we're each perceived individually within a digital landscape. It's been long enough that I've realized what time can do to the Weird and the people like myself who interact with it and publicly share that on the internet.

Two things, really:

People will come and go, start and stop, be there and then gone... a lot: teams, individuals, brands, even places. There isn't a category of person involved in the paranormal that is exempt, and it happens for any and every reason. After this amount of time, it's just a bizarre realization to have watched it happen and see so many people slip in and out of an intent to push the boundaries of reality with investigating and pursuit of Fortean moments. It makes me realize how many more people are invested in the paranormal, for whatever motivation they might have, than I would have expected to see. Without the ability to connect across so many digital spaces, I'd still be viewing the same desktop forums and websites I was viewing before I owned a hand computer named after a fruit connected to billions of people. The rise and fall of paranormal participation is real. "Nothing gold can stay."

Age matters. It matters in a distinct way for women in and out of the paranormal. Age is inseparable from the social architecture we've been maintaining for the systems of capitalism and patriarchy to remain in place.

> THESE SYSTEMS WERE BUILT CENTURIES BEFORE US, BUT THEY CREATED WOUNDS THAT BLEED FOREVER INTO OUR PRESENT, AND AS OF NOW, INTO OUR FORESEEABLE FUTURE.

This isn't new information to most people—it's just a realization within myself and my *own* age and how *my* public presentation/acceptance/worth is affected within the public paranormal community.

To begin with, the start and stop of so many people in the paranormal, authentic investigators and entertainers both, is not very absurd or as profound as the second factor. The age thing is unreasonably brutal, though, and I'm a woman, so this one is a shot to the gut.

A line from Rebecca Jennings' 2020 article in *Vox* was poignant:

"It's... impossible to talk about the fear of aging without talking about the precise terror that it represents for women. Our worth is inseparable from our youth, so much so that embracing the effects of time is considered a radical act."

The agency and worth of women wane as we increase in age. This speaks to women outside of any niche interest or community, but within the paranormal and the spiritual, witchcraft, and horror communities, and online, where all those interests intersect, it's just as apparent.

> ONE WOULD LIKE TO ASSUME THAT THE OLDER THE PERSON IS, THE MORE THEY MIGHT BE RESPECTED FOR WHAT THEY'VE GAINED IN YEARS OF EXPERIENCE... BUT THAT'S NOT THE DESIGN. THAT'S NOT THE SYSTEM OR WHAT IT FEEDS ON.

I know this sounds extremely negative, and so far, we're all on the bleeding edge of rage, screaming for too many valid reasons, but bear with me.

After being present for over a decade of paranormal social media and having a public presence on the internet, I see where the peak is climbed and attained easier than ever before. It has become easier to spot where real value is present in the noise of so much spooky content. I've also noticed that with age, I gain more of a sense of contentment and fully realized, valued relationships are worked on with intent and purpose. The wide amalgam of friends dwindles to the most authentic, important, and closest, and there's no need to waste energy on anyone that doesn't positively impact me and my work. I feel less obligation to peripheral interactions with those who circulate the same spaces to "stay relevant" or "play nice." We teach kids to "play nice with others," now it's just more like, "if it's not enriching my experience, no need to engage." That simplicity helps to maintain a sense of peace. In a world that seems to be filling more and more with noise and a discord of curated content, I've found that approaching the online aspect of the paranormal with patience and contemplation is more necessary than I'd have ever thought.

When I was younger and still fresh at spending hours in the dark with hopes of experiencing a ghost, I was quicker to anger and quicker to take sides in a field that doesn't seem to have clear sides anywhere. I used to feel compelled to appear as perhaps more than I really was then, to take the place of the helplessness of being a beginner in so many aspects of the paranormal. I can see that in my younger investigator self with a bit more clarity now. And cringing.

I can only guess that it's due simply to the omnipresence of the social platforms we've become cogs in the machine of, but having time to reflect on being a woman in this field has made it less disheartening as I come to understand what I've gained. As much as I can see my youth and my value tied intrinsically together, and see it working its way into lesser available spaces for me as I age, I see the other side too. No, I don't mean I'm closer to death. I mean that I'm becoming comfortable realizing with age comes the insight and knowledge I've gained—books read, places visited, experiences had, people met, world views and perspectives expanded, imploded, and built again because enough time has gone by for me to accumulate those things now.

There's a reverence in the passage of years when they form a foundation of understanding and reflection instead of ego. The other thing is the sense of comfort in the unknown and enjoying the mystery of not having answers that I like to talk about too much—I'd never be able to have that in my 20s. I certainly wouldn't have been able to gain objective insight into my beliefs, skepticisms, and interactions with the paranormal as those moments unfolded. But I didn't know that then. I hadn't lived enough to know, and I didn't have these years and their aftereffects and lessons yet.

Full disclosure: sometimes life's lessons are wretched. They're full of liars, haters, takers, the creepy kind of weirdos, jealous jerks, users, abusers, and the ever-present grifters. Terrible teachers, valuable lessons. When I say I'm keeping this within the paranormal, I do mean that all those nasty people are absolutely to be found within this community. The very pliable nature of unknownness can be utilized by anyone in so many ways, and not all have honest means to honest ends. It's hard to navigate that community, be female, and just exist all at once.

It's a rich experience being a woman in the paranormal, especially now a decade into content creation and public online spaces. With the female experience in Western society being embattled in the outward visibility of youth and appearance, it can be a nightmare to exist in digital spaces designed to exploit any lack of those as vulnerabilities. There is no way to single-handedly break apart this cruel aspect of society and publicity, but I believe there is a way through it. It ties in with the first thing I mentioned, the come-and-go nature of so many people involved in the paranormal.

The way through is remaining present in the purpose of the endeavor. Staying enthralled with (and curious to experience) the paranormal with those you love and friends who are also Very Weird, and reexamining the unexplained situations you go through as they accumulate are what I keep finding to be the most gratifying part. It's like realizing the portion of a race that involves sprinting is over, and now it's a comfortable pace without the distractions of unnecessary competition or overt societal expectations. The creation and the actions of what we do, and how we remain curious and experiment and move forward in the paranormal have always been the most important aspect for me personally, but they're becoming less clouded by peripheral noise.

My age being a worth-based calculator becomes something I've begun to weigh as more time goes by, but barring any medical circumstances, we all age at the same pace and my number happens to be 38 right now. I don't necessarily need to swipe open Instagram and post a filter-less photo of my under-eye duffle bags in a radical protest against the patriarchy, but I do not feel the same sense of urgency in being exactly what I know is expected and wanted of me as a woman.

IT LEAVES ROOM FOR WHAT'S MOST EXCITING: THE ACTUAL PARANORMAL.

Being able to better assess where real value is present in the people, concepts, places, and work being done in the field is a process that takes time and still remains fluid, but that's what these years of being here in it all and being a public person has given me, and can give anyone. Focusing on those values fuels the important parts of this entire undertaking of investigating and studying the Strange and Unusual, including navigating digital media as a female human being, which can be, as you know, horrifying.

The paranormal road has a lot of sprinters, walkers, wanderers, curious bystanders, and more, joining or leaving the community constantly. I'm rapidly graying, and my knee joints become audible with particular movements, but I'm remaining firmly on that same road, invested in odd things I can't explain and just want to know more about. There will always be weak points and places along the way where, like any woman, I'll question my worth as this journey continues.

Being able to reflect back with knowledge and experience, keeping admirable people around me, learning from those before me, and supporting those who merge onto this road after me are how I believe I can surpass that, and where I believe true power can be sourced for the good of this weird, bizarre, frustrating, intriguing community of the paranormal, even in public digital spaces where so much of our interaction takes place now. It just takes time.

THE CURIOUS HISTORY OF CORPSE CANDLES

Kate Cherrell

One of the most fascinating supernatural legends of the British Isles is that of the corpse candle. Originating in Wales in the 18th and 19th Centuries, corpse candles were considered an omen of death, feared, and developed over centuries of folkloric tradition. Otherwise known as the *Canwyll Corph* or *Canwyllau Cryff*, corpse candles are neither made from corpses nor corpse wax [Corpse wax, otherwise known as adipocere, is a waxy substance that builds up from the anaerobic bacterial hydrolysis of fat in body tissue.], but are harbingers of death. As a light that predicts the death of an individual, corpse candles are variations on the traditions of "spooklights" and "earthlights," which are occasional, mythical, or supernatural emissions of light.

The notion of a corpse candle is an inextricably Welsh phenomenon, as interlinked with the nation's landscape as the patron saint who confirmed their existence. Legend dictates that in life, St. David sought to ease the concerns of his parish, who were anxious that loved ones would pass away without their knowledge. David took their concerns to heart and prayed that the Lord would see fit to ease their worries. God duly answered and decreed that any imminent death in Wales would be marked by a visible sign—a ball of light, gradually dimming as it approached their place of death. David's position as an intercessor with God soon established his sainthood and importance to the proud nation.

> ### SAINTS NOTWITHSTANDING, WITH CORPSE CANDLES, SIZE IS EVERYTHING.

The size of the candle represents the age of the person about to die—if the candle is short, they are young, if the candle is long, they are old. It's a simple and effective system, easily remembered across classes and cultures. If two candles appear together, with one shorter than the other, the deaths will be those of a mother and child. If the candle flame is red, the deceased will be a man. If the flame is white, it will be a woman. Regional variations are to be expected, but this visual shorthand has maintained its longevity in Welsh folklore throughout the years.

Corpse candles were also mobile, not appearing in the same terrestrial space each time. They relate to corpse roads, which were used for hundreds of years and are similarly self-explanatory, referring to the old roads used to take bodies to the church or burial ground. In many instances, corpse candles were reported as small lights that lingered on these roads at night, signaling either souls that had already passed through the roads, or those about to travel down them.

One Welsh woman's story, reported in *British Goblins* by Wirt Sikes (1880), reads as follows:

One night her sister was lying very ill at the [Welsh woman's] house, and [the sister] was alone with her children, her husband being in the lunatic asylum at Cardiff. She had just put the children to bed and had set the candle on the floor preparatory to going to bed herself when there came a 'swish' along the floor like the rustling of graves clothes [shrouds], and the candle was blown out. The room, however, to her surprise remained glowing with a feeble light as from a very small taper, and looking behind her, she beheld 'old John Richards' who had been dead ten years. He held a corpse candle in his hand, and he looked at her in a chill and steadfast manner, which caused blood to run cold in her veins. She turned and woke her eldest boy, and said to him, "Don't you see old John Richards?" The boy asked, "Where?" rubbing his eyes. She pointed out the ghost, and the boy was so frightened at the sight of it that he cried out, "Oh, wi! Oh, dduw! I wish I may die!" The ghost then disappeared, the Corpse Candle in its hand; the candle on the floor burned again with a clear light, and the next day the sick sister died.

Another story from a man named Thomas Matthews recounts the horrifying image of a corpse candle burning inside his father's mouth, stretching to his feet, before retracting and disappearing back into his mouth shortly before the man died. A 1979 interview preserved by the *National Museum of Wales* records a man from Ysbyty Ystwyth recounting his grandfather's experiences with corpse candles:

He'd had many experiences of the corpse candle. My grandmother died when my mother was eight years old, my Uncle David six, and Aunty Charlotte a baby, a young girl, twenty-eight years old. She died of the dicâd [tuberculosis], as they called it in those days, [and] there was no cure. And the night before she died, he was by her bedside, and he saw a little lighted candle on the bed, and he saw it going out of the house. And then his wife died. And he saw his wife's corpse candle going out of the house. And she saw it too. She said:

"Do you see that light going out through the door, Tomos?" Both she and he saw the light, and she died the next day.

In a report from London, hospital staff reported seeing a blue flame emanate from inside a man's mouth shortly before death. However, critics of the story believe this to have been ignited hydrogen, resulting from the decomposition of the man's body.

As such, corpse candles weren't necessarily candle-shaped; they could appear as balls of light and even be accompanied by a human skull, compounding the inescapable deathly links of the supernatural candle. In other accounts, a cluster of corpse candles seen in mid-air signaled a death in a nearby house. Alternatively, such a sight may indicate that the individual witnessing them was going to die.

Corpse candles did not only signal the death of an individual, but traced the path their body would take. These deathly candles could travel "over mountains, valleys, even rivers, and marshland, never bothering with traditional routes and seeming to be able to travel wherever they wished."

One such traveling candle story comes from Maurice Griffiths, a Baptist preacher and former schoolmaster of Pontfaen in Pembrokeshire. Griffiths saw a red light in the valley below as he walked by at night. He saw the red light travel before stopping motionless for 15 minutes, then continuing its journey to the church and churchyard of Llanferch-Llawddog Church. Days later, the young son of a man named Peter Higgon of Pontfaen died, and the child's funeral procession took the same route as the corpse light. As with the flame, the funeral procession had to wait for 15 minutes at a body of water while they received help to move the coffin across. The child was eventually buried in the same spot where the corpse candle had lingered before disappearing.

Few collectors of folk tales tried to rationalize or explain the roots of the corpse candle. However, in an account from 1848, the writer states that corpse candles:

> *Seem to be of electrical origin, when the ears of the traveller's horse, the extremity of his whip, his spurs, or any other projecting points appear tipped with pencils of light... the toes of the rider's boots, and even the tufts of hair at the fetlocks of his horse, appeared to burn with a steady blue light, and on the hand being extended, every finger immediately became tipped with fire.*

Sussex folklorist Charlotte Latham hypothesized that accounts of corpse candles could be misinterpretations of glowworms, which—

although rather more corporeal—has been a theory of little consequence to the engrained folk tradition.

Corpse candles make up just one small part of Welsh death folklore and were often seen as a component of ghost or phantom funerals, where spectral funeral processions made their way down corpse roads, accompanied by the sound of weeping mourners.

With industrialization came the decline of folk beliefs and superstitions across Wales and the wider landscape of the United Kingdom, but the terrifying ominous flame of a corpse candle has never truly been extinguished.

References:

Via Spencer, John and Jane. The Encyclopedia of Ghosts and Spirits. BCA. 1992.

https://museum.wales/collections/folktales/?story=15

https://www.bbc.co.uk/blogs/wales/entries/7a238820-7a42-35c4-93b1-118530e88167

James Motley. *Notes to the Canwyll Corph*. London: Longmans, and Hughes; Swansea: Brewster; and Llanelly: Thomas. pp.112-115. 1848.

DRAWING THE DEAD: A BEGINNER'S GUIDE TO PSYCHIC ART

Jenny Pugh

I'd like you to study the portrait below. Please look carefully at the mystery lady's face. She had curly, dark hair and arched eyebrows. She wore earrings and loved scarves. Look in her eyes and ask yourself, *Does this look and sound like someone I know?* Is this the portrait of someone you once knew but is now in the spirit world?

I am sure that someone reading this journal *will* recognize them, for this is a psychic portrait drawn during meditation connected to my spirit guides. I decided to challenge myself (and my guides) to draw a spirit portrait of someone I knew nothing about but that one reader of *The Feminine Macabre* would recognize. Could you be that person? Was this psychic portrait meant for you*?*

Being a clairvoyant medium, I can communicate with the spirit world, but I can also draw the spirits that visit me, such as spirit guides and those who have passed away (such as the pastel drawing below). The term for this mediumistic ability is "psychic artist," a unique art form as the artist connects with the divine to produce their ultimate creation. As Leonardo da Vinci famously said, "Where the spirit does not work with the hand, there is no art."

Psychic art has been popular for many years. It became prevalent during the golden age of Spiritualism (from the mid-19th to mid-20th Century) when a remarkable surge in its scientific study came about. Many Victorian scientists and philosophers were fascinated by spiritual mediums purporting to contact the dead, and psychic artwork became significant evidence to those investigating the work of mediums, such as London-based spiritualist Georgina Houghton. She famously produced automatic pencil drawings and abstract watercolors inspired by spirit. Her artwork was later publicly exhibited and drew large crowds.

There are many types of psychic art, not just the spiritual portraiture of those who have passed away. Some mediums produce abstract works inspired by spiritual visions, and others draw colorful auragraphs. These (often circular) symbolic drawings are said to represent a person's past, present, and future potential. They were initially developed by British medium Harold Sharpe, who coined the term "auragraph."

Sharpe's interest in Spiritualism began when he visited The Psychic Bookshop, a bookstore and museum founded by Sherlock Holmes's author and keen Spiritualist, Sir Arthur Conan Doyle. Sharpe toured British Spiritualist churches demonstrating his abilities. He would interpret his client's aura with the help of his Chinese spirit guide and draw colorful symbols and shapes to complete the auragraph drawing. He would then relate the artwork's meaning to his sitter. As with many psychic artists (myself included), Sharpe worked quickly in getting the image down on paper.

Another talented promoter of this form of mediumship was the late Coral Polge, who once demonstrated her art at the Royal Albert Hall in London. This British medium, aided by her spirit guide, Maurice Quentin de la Tour (a renowned French pastel portrait artist), demonstrated her artistic abilities on stage while accompanied by another medium who directed the messages. Coral is said to have completed over 50,000 portraits of those who had passed to spirit.

Spirit connections can be very brief, as spirit guides can "download" a lot of information into the mind of a medium very quickly. When drawing spirit-inspired artwork, you generally don't have much time. Instead, you are trying to catch the elusive spirit images that flit through your mind while working with the other side. This fleeting information can comprise glimpses of a subject's face, voice fragments, and additional information about their character and lifestyle. It's a very different process to drawing a still life, such as a bowl of fruit or a vase of flowers, that will stay in place for as long as you need to complete your sketch. The information needs to be captured quickly while the connection with spirit is in full flow, and drawing with pastels (such as the portrait of my guide on the previous page) or soft artist pencils is an excellent way of achieving this.

If you'd like to try psychic art yourself, don't worry, you don't need to be artistic—anyone can try it. You'll also need little in the way of materials, at least to start with. A beginner only needs the basics, a pencil or a pen, some paper, a bit of time, and a quiet space to work. If you enjoy the process or are particularly talented, you can always invest in better materials later. You can choose to use any drawing medium for psychic portraiture, but pick one you feel most comfortable using (you can always experiment later). You can choose to work in monochrome or color—I would recommend working in black and white for a beginner, as you can use one pencil and don't have to keep changing drawing materials during the full flow of your drawing session.

If you choose to sketch in black and white, graphite pencils make a great choice. You can mix and match a variety of leads allowing you to get tonal effects in your work (a 2b, 4b, 6b, and 8b would be perfect for this). Pencil drawings are also more straightforward as they don't require fixing (with fixative spray), which pastel portraits usually require. You could equally use a pen to draw, but you wouldn't have the fantastic range of mark-making that sketching pencils afford an artist. If you prefer to draw in ink, consider using a Fudenosuke brush pen to allow more line expression.

If you wish to work in color, there are many drawing mediums, such as colored pencils or watercolors. However, I would recommend the "medium's medium," namely pastels. Many psychic artists favor pastels when drawing, as they are quick to apply to the paper and are easy to blend. I recommend using them for speed, as you can cover a lot of paper in just a few seconds.

Pastels range significantly in quality and price. But, if possible, invest in or borrow good-quality artist pastels, as you will find them easier to use and produce better results. My favorites are *Conté à Paris* pastels, which have a solid feel for drawing and excellent color coverage. If you are using pastels, you will also need some *Ingres* paper (or similar paper with a rough surface) to draw on so that the paper holds the color well. Working with color can also help build your knowledge and interpretations of colors received from spirit, including the colors of the aura.

As I work on replicating a spirit person's portrait, I also keep a pencil handy to jot down at the side of the picture quick notes on any information I've picked up clairvoyantly, such as names, places, or character traits connected to the subject of the study. This brief notation saves precious seconds. I can revisit the notes later to remind myself what spirit was saying and write this  in more detail for my client. For example, I once tuned into Spirit and produced the portrait of a woman (see above) wearing a fashionable hat and a string of green beads. I nicknamed her The Bee Lady, as my guides informed me that she'd been a keen beekeeper when alive.

While drawing her, I found a myriad of information flowing so quickly that it was hard to keep it in mind. So, I jotted notes down on the side of the drawing, to which I could later refer. I recommend you leave an area of your page free to make such notes when doing your portrait.

Once you are ready to start drawing, sit comfortably and place your drawing materials in front of you. Close your eyes and ask your spirit guides to step forward and help you create a psychic drawing. You can either do this out loud or, if you prefer, think it. Your guides are telepathic and will be able to read your thoughts. Say something like, "I call on my spirit guides to step forward and give me protection and healing, and work with me to produce a portrait of one of my guides." You can always tweak the wording so that it feels comfortable to you. When working with Spirit, it isn't the exact words you say but your intention that is important. Luckily, your guides will know what you intend to do ahead of time and will be ready to help facilitate the process.

Next, please pick up your pencil (or pastel), and place it on the paper. Relax and imagine Spirit's influence flowing through your body and into your hand. Let your imagination go and draw whatever comes to mind, don't be restricted by negative thoughts or feelings that you are doing the wrong thing, as there is no wrong thing, only the right way. Try to feel what your guide looks like. Sketch the shape of their head, eyes, and the outline of their nose and lips. Draw faintly to begin and strengthen your line as you feel more confident.

In your mind, ask your spirit guide about their hair, whether it is wavy or long, whether they have any hair, or wear a hat. Do they have a beard, mustache, or wear glasses? Be watchful for snippets of ideas that form in your mind—this is your guide doing what they do best, guiding you to the correct answer. You may find that a name, previous occupation, favorite hobby, or place of birth also pops into your mind. If so, jot it down. Drawing in this way is a personal way to connect with your spirit guides. It helps you learn about each other and how to connect and work together. It is a fantastic process and an excellent way to develop your psychic potential.

Once you feel you have completed your portrait, please take a good look at it, and thank your guides for working with you to produce their picture. Now break your connection, get back to normal, and ground yourself. Put your pencil down, stretch your legs, have a drink or a bite to eat, and carry on with your day—and don't forget to congratulate yourself on having just taken the first steps in becoming a psychic artist!

Oh, and that portrait I showed you initially—did you recognize them? If you think so, I'd love you to get in touch at www.jennypughpsychic.com!

Haunted Dolls:
Your Friend 'Til the End

Ariana Rose

Just the thought of haunted dolls paints images in our minds from films such as *Child's Play*, *Annabelle*, and *The Boy*. Hollywood loves to entertain (and frighten) us with stories of cursed or haunted dolls… but did you know there are real examples of paranormal activity surrounding dolls all over the United States?

Laffing Sal

Standing at the height of six-feet, ten-inches, Laffing Sal has been known to terrorize children (and even some adults) who come in contact with her. Before I get into just how creepy she is (and believe me: she's creepy), let's see who Sal is, the story of her creation, and what makes her so terrifying.

Sal was created by the Philadelphia Toboggan Company as one of several animatronics used to attract people to carnivals and amusement parks throughout the United States in the 1930s. Today, Sal has become something of an icon among haunted dolls, making an appearance in *The Princess Diaries* and several other films.

Sal has unruly ginger locks and freckles drawn on her face. There are a variety of versions of Sal with different outfits, but only one is haunted, and she wears a floral dress and lives in the Ocean City Lifesaving Station Museum. Sal's main attraction was that she laughed when a button was pressed. The laugh track was initially played on a record and a tape in later years… This button will be highly significant later in Sal's tale.

At first, Sal had moderate success drawing in crowds like the rest of the animatronics, but her fame soon grew to infamy. Many people felt she was creepy, but they never suspected her of being involved in paranormal activity until employees started to experience unusual things around her.

Workers reported hearing Sal laugh when no one had pressed the button and even when she was unplugged. To make this pure nightmare fuel, the pitch of her laughter is said to be very deep and not the laugh of a female—an older man actually recorded the laugh.

There have been countless reports of hearing Sal laugh when she is not on or when her button has not been pressed. Many employees and visitors at the Ocean City Lifesaving Station Museum have reported seeing a full-body apparition of a young, blond boy. He is quite famous, wearing 1930s-Era clothing, and is said to appear so clearly that workers search for his parents. Has this spirit attached himself to Sal? Could he be the one pressing Sal's button, making her laugh?

The museum is a location that is no stranger to loss since it served as a lifesaving station for many years. Perhaps it was one of the many sailors who lost their lives in the waters, too late to be saved.

ROBERT THE DOLL

Robert the Doll could be the most famous doll in the world. Robert has inspired numerous films about haunted dolls, including *Annabelle*, *Child's Play*, and even his own movie in 2015, entitled simply, *Robert*.

The year was 1904 when Robert Eugene Otto was gifted a life-size doll. Some stories say his grandfather gave him the doll, but local legend claims a family servant gave it to him. Some locals believe it was given as a retaliation for a wrongdoing and was cursed. Either way, Robert Eugene was the first person to have Robert in his possession. Robert became obsessed with the doll and named it after himself. His obsession went as far as to build the doll its own room with furniture and toys, including the gift of Robert's iconic teddy bear.

As the young boy matured, he would blame the doll for any mistakes or wrongdoings he himself made. Eventually, the doll became more of a punching bag than a companion. As all do, Robert Eugene grew up and eventually became engaged to a woman named Anne. When Robert Eugene came home to his parents' house, Robert the Doll was there waiting for him, having spent his time in those days propped up against a window.

The first reports of Robert the Doll being haunted came from local children walking home from school—they would look in the window and report seeing the doll move from one side of the window to the other. Some people who visited the home describe how the doll's expressions changed according to whatever the people in the room were talking about. One of the most common reports was the sound of giggling from Robert when no one else was in the room.

Anne, Robert Eugene's wife, hated the doll and demanded that he be locked in a cedar chest in their attic upon her husband's death. Many years after Anne's death, a group of civilians exploring the home discovered Robert. They donated him to the Key West Art and Historical Society.

Today, he is on display at the East Martello Museum. Most people believe he is malicious and will curse you and your loved ones.

Personally, I think whatever spirit possesses Robert was neglected during Robert Eugene's ownership and simply wants attention.

THE DOLLS' HOUSE GALLERY

It's a truth that seems to be acknowledged by the paranormal community that dolls can be haunted, but paranormal attachments sometimes extend beyond dolls to their tiny houses.

The Mildred M. Mahoney Dolls' House Gallery, located in Fort Erie, Canada, hosted a collection of over 140 dollhouses—built between 1780 and 1995—and some paranormal activity as well.

The house in which the museum resided was built in 1835 by the Forsyth family and remained in the family's care until 1865.

According to stories, there was a tunnel in the basement of the home to assist with the Underground Railroad. It's believed the son of Mr. Forsyth lost his life by drowning in the tunnel. In his grief, Forsyth ordered the tunnel to be sealed up.

Mildred Mahoney was the wife of a prominent lawyer in the region. Ever since she was a little girl, she had loved dollhouses, and as an adult, she began to collect them. When her husband passed away in 1982, she purchased the Forsyth Mansion and turned it into a museum for her beloved collection.

When people visited the museum, they sometimes felt an intense pressure bearing down on them. The aesthetic of the place was eerie. Empty dollhouses discarded by children who have long since grown up and passed away. Some of the dollhouses were made of matches, and even one was made from a bathroom cabinet. The houses came from all over the world—the United States, Canada, England, and Japan.

One dollhouse was particularly affected and liked to move on its own. If the workers returned the house to its original spot, they would come back the following day to find it back in the same place where it was before they had moved it. The house was locked up tight at night, with no one allowed in, but the dollhouse would somehow find its way back to that spot each time. The curator said that a psychic told them that the room with the dollhouse happened to be the bedroom of Mr. Forsyth's son, who passed away, and that he preferred it to be on the side of the room where a dollhouse was located when he was alive. The haunted dollhouse also happened to have a miniature Ouija board in one of its rooms.

In 1991, when Mildred Mahoney passed away, the museum was believed to host the most extensive dollhouse collection in the world. Soon, paranormal investigators recorded a woman's voice in the museum that workers identified as Mrs. Mahoney, adding to the supernatural occurrences in the museum.

Sadly, the museum closed in 2010, and the dollhouses were sold. It is not known if the activity continues with the new owners. Is the house itself haunted by the tragic death of Mr. Forsyth's son? Or were the vintage dollhouses haunted objects that stirred up energy in the Mildred M. Mahoney Dolls' House Gallery?

What is the connection between dolls and otherworldly activity? Do ghostly presences find it easier to attach themselves to human-like dolls?

> ARE CHILDREN'S PLAYTHINGS MORE SUSCEPTIBLE BECAUSE CHILDREN ARE MORE OPEN TO PARANORMAL ACTIVITY?

Many times children see apparitions, claim they are imaginary friends, and sometimes have other encounters that parents simply blame on their imaginations.

Perhaps haunted dolls are simply an extension of this.

References:

Butler, Brooke (2018, October) *Haunted Delmarva Ocean City Life Saving Station Museum* Retrieved April, 2022 https://www.wmdt.com/2018/10/haunted-delmarva-ocean-city-life-saving-station-museum/

Shorebread (2011, October) *Haunted History Ocean City Life Saving Station Museum Locals Week Featuring Shipwrecks and Spirits* Retrieved April, 2022 https://shorebread.com/2011/10/24/haunted-history-ocean-city-life-saving-station-museum-locals-week-featuring-shipwrecks-and-spirits/

Artist House Key West (2022) *Discover the Story of Robert the Doll* Retrieved April 2022 https://www.artisthousekeywest.com/robert-the-doll

Buffalo News Staff (1991, January) *Mildred M Mahoney Dies at 72 Renowned for Dollhouse Museum* Retrieved April, 2022 https://buffalonews.com/news/mildred-m-mahoney-dies-at-72-renowned-for-dollhouse-collection/article_f9f0d9d5-e101-555a-9f1f-1bceb2b3e2d5.html

Chris Mills (2010, "Winter") *This is the End: Mildred Mahoney's Dollhouse Collection* Retrieved April 2022 http://www.neviews.ca/Samples/13%20mahoney.pdf

Brian Baker (2021, January) *Could Fort Erie's Bertie Hall Just Be One Big Haunted Dollhouse?* Retrieved April, 2022 https://www.superstitioustimes.com/could-fort-eries-bertie-hall-hold-secrets-from-underground-railroad/

Death Views and Postmortem Photography

Alyssa Vang and
Tamora L Vang

Trigger Warning: This article includes postmortem photographs of the dead, including children.

How do you feel about death and dying? If you were to pose this question to your great-grandparents, you might find their answers to be wildly dissimilar to your own.

In the days of our ancestors, death was part of everyday life. Most people did not go to hospitals to die—they were either too expensive or too far away. Instead, families cared for their relatives in their own homes until they drew their last precious breath.

Children were present in the home to experience the process of death, even observing how the deceased was lovingly cleaned, clothed, and laid out in the parlor for viewings.

Through social change in the 19th and 20th Centuries, there have been influences on rituals, customs, memorials, and mourning observed for the death of a loved one. In the 21st Century, society has begun to send our aged and infirmed to hospitals and homes to spend their last days—so much of modern American society envisions the process of death as unknown or unseen. Postmortem rituals have been dismissed as morbid and therefore have been kept private for any who might still carry out such practices.

One of the many traditions in the wake of a death performed during the 19th and 20th Centuries included postmortem photography.

Postmortem photography grew in popularity when the camera was invented in 1816 (specifically the daguerreotype in 1839). Since death was part of every household, postmortem photography was embraced by the masses.

Previously, death memorial portraits had only been available to the rich by commissioning expensive portraits, but daguerreotypes made it possible for the lower and middle class to memorialize their loved ones using this new and cheaper option. These photographs were often the only way someone of a lower class would have a picture of their loved ones. Like painted portraits, the deceased was dressed in their finest, such as a confirmation or wedding gown. There were also items,  such as flowers and toys included in the photographs to make it appear as if they were still alive and engaging in activities they enjoyed.

At that time, there was a long wait while the photograph was exposed. Since the dead didn't move, that was an advantage for photographers of postmortem photography as it was easier to take their pictures. Often, the deceased posed by themselves, standing (with the help of a stand) or sitting on a chair, which put them in a more natural pose to make it seem as if they were still alive. With children, sometimes a parent—usually the mother—wore a veil and sat with the child on their lap. There were also times other family members were included in the portraits, either to help prop up the deceased or simply to have this one opportunity to have a family photo taken with their loved one.

Photographers found there were times that it was difficult to prop up the deceased due to natural gravity, but rigor-mortis sometimes played a role in keeping the subject in a pose. The photographer had to try and account for decomposition by closing the eyes and painting over the eyelids to make them appear as if they were open.

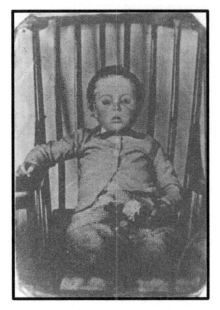

In some cases, the purpose of taking postmortem photographs was more than just family memorials. In the days of the old west, postmortem photographs were used as not only proof of death for people to receive the "dead or alive" reward for infamous outlaws, but they also served as warnings to those who might dare cross the lines of the law. Sometimes that postmortem photo of an outlaw was merely a trophy.

By the end of the 19th and early 20th Century, the practice of posing the deceased as if they were alive was ending. After this time, the postmortem photos began to have more obvious death poses, such as the dead in a coffin or laying down with closed eyes while the family stood around them.

This practice continued until World War II, when more people had access to cameras. These days we all have devices like cell phones and tablets where we have taken and stored hundreds or thousands of photos of our loved ones. These serve as memorials of life and not just death, so postmortem photography is no longer needed for most of us. However, it has become popular now with families who experience the death of a baby.

Now I Lay Me Down to Sleep is a website that partners skilled photographers with families who want a remembrance gift of a professional photograph. Photographers, retouch artists, and medical affiliates volunteer their time and services to help grieving families memorialize their babies through remembrance photography.

We also find forward-thinking people like Caitlin Doughty stepping up to educate us all about death. With their help, our views of mortality and death are changing, and we're starting to plan and execute funerals for ourselves or our loved ones. Caitlin, a mortician and an advocate for death acceptance and the reform of Western funeral industry practices, along with her group, The Order of the Good Death, focuses on solutions for the current view of death and provides support for alternative forms of death care.

Whatever your current view on death may be, take the time to educate yourself on the possibilities available so your wishes and those of your loved ones are fulfilled.

References:

"Victorian Death Art: Postmortem Death Photography and Hair Art" by
Emily Ann Bronte

"Beyond the Dark Veil: Post Mortem & Mourning Photography From The
Thanatos Archive" by Jack Mord

Bad Influence from the Studio of Lisa Volrath (zine); October 2006 issue.
"Photography: A Dead Issue"

https://en.wikipedia.org/wiki/Post-mortem_photography

http://www.thehorrorzine.com/Morbid/VictorianPostMortemPhotography.h
tml

Now I Lay Me Down to Sleep website:
https://www.nowilaymedowntosleep.org/

THE WINCHESTER DAISY: A COCKTAIL INSPIRED BY SARAH WINCHESTER AND HER FAVORITE FLOWER

Chelsea Celaya

The combined histories of the Winchester Mystery House and the development of alcoholic spirits in San Jose lend a strong hand in inspiring the creation of this beautiful cocktail I have dubbed the "Winchester Daisy." Fresh, natural ingredients make this cocktail shine best, with orange and lemon adding mystery to what is hidden inside this bright libation, much like exploring the halls of the Winchester Mystery House itself.

Ingredients

- 2 ounces Winchester Kentucky Straight Bourbon Whiskey
- 1 ounce lemon juice *(fresh squeezed)*
- ½ ounce orange juice *(fresh squeezed)*
- ½ ounce simple syrup
- Champagne to top
- Edible chrysanthemum or fleabane flowers *(optional for garnish)*

Tools Needed

- Cocktail shaker
- Jigger
- Juicer
- Lowball cocktail glass
- One ice ball or cube

Instructions

1. Fill cocktail shaker halfway with ice
2. Add whiskey, lemon juice, orange juice, and simple syrup to cocktail shaker
3. Shake vigorously until shaker feels frosted
4. Add ice ball to lowball glass
5. Strain mix from cocktail shaker into lowball glass
6. Top with champagne
7. Garnish with flower
8. Enjoy!

Alcoholic and Spectral Cocktail Research

Known to Sarah Winchester as *Llanada Villa,* The Winchester Mystery House began receiving its first visitors only five months after Sarah's death on September 5, 1922. Today, it still calls out to the curious-minded, eager to enchant its next guests. Keen-eyed visitors of Sarah Winchester's Victorian home may notice repeating motifs throughout the house depicting her favorite flower, the daisy. These can be seen in just about everything, from the stained-glass windows to the window locks, to door handles, and even the wallpaper. Wander the gardens outside and you cannot miss the fresh daisies growing throughout the property.

Detail of stained-glass daisy-patterned window, Winchester House, 1933.
Photo courtesy of National Parks Service

While Sarah oversaw the constant construction of her San Jose farmhouse into the quizzical mansion we know today, the city was experiencing its own liquor industry growth. There was a high demand for readily available alcoholic spirits as saloons and taverns sprung up around the Santa Clara valley. The more popular and requested spirits were influenced by the immigrants moving into California, including beer from the Germans, wine from the Italians, and whiskey from those on the East Coast heading West.

Armed with the above knowledge of both the Winchester Mystery House and the liquor boom occurring in the Bay Area in the 1800s, I drew on my resources to design a cocktail worthy of Sarah's name. Thankfully, a delightful Kentucky bourbon whiskey, also named "Winchester," was already part of my liquor cabinet. This served as the starting point for crafting this cocktail. Personally, I am not a big bourbon whiskey person. However, during my research for bourbon cocktails, I stumbled across a traditional recipe called a "Bourbon Daisy," a twist on the "Whiskey Sour," which used bourbon, lemon juice, sugar, and grenadine. The ingredients felt simple enough to experiment creatively with. After some minor adjustments, I ended up with the cocktail you see here. The combination presented in this cocktail is perfect for both novice and seasoned cocktail drinkers. The orange compliments the sweetness of the bourbon, while the champagne brings out the whiskey's more subtle flavors to end with a bubbly finish on your tongue.

The Winchester Mystery House
Photo courtesy of Www78

Ready to try a hand at this cocktail? If so, then grab your glass because, in the presumed words of Sarah Winchester, it is time to "build when the spirits move you!"

HALLOWED AND HUSHED BE THE PLACES OF THE DEAD

Stephanie Bingham

Strange sights litter the backroads. A summer drive can lead to many odd discoveries. One of my most unexpected was in the oldest town in Kentucky, the tiny city of Harrodsburg.

While lost on my way to Old Fort Harrod, I came across a charming city park with a large, wooden playground for children, a pavilion for cookouts, and something that seemed out of place. Right next to the small parking lot sat a short white fence, conveniently enclosing an area about the size of a grave. I was sure I wasn't seeing what I thought I was, so I parked and investigated. It was indeed a grave with a full slab over the burial area, but the monument at the head of the grave conveniently did not have a name or any dates inscribed on it. Instead, the grave of the unfortunate reads:

Unknown
Hallowed and
Hushed be the
Places of the Dead
Step softly,
Bow Head

As it turns out, this area was famous for what many small towns in the region were known for—mineral springs. Before the advent of what we know as truly modern medicine, thousands of health spas across the country would use mineral baths, hot springs, and the waters in them to treat everything from exhaustion to tuberculosis. It didn't take long for the spas and hotels around them to start drawing crowds looking for relaxation and a change of scenery. That is exactly what happened in Harrodsburg.

In the early 1800s, the Graham Springs Hotel, later known as the Harrodsburg Springs Hotel, was built in the location of the modern-day park to take advantage of the local mineral springs. The area became known as the "Saratoga of the West" and was an extremely popular destination for tourists looking to relax and enjoy the spas. This particular hotel was known to attract a very upscale crowd due to its ballrooms and proximity to railways.

In the warm summer of 1840, a young woman checked into the hotel under the name of Victoria Stafford, the daughter of a prominent Louisville judge. She was, by all accounts, a lovely young woman in her early 20s traveling alone with a trunk. She was excited to partake in the festivities found at the hotel. Victoria appeared in the darkened ballroom that evening and danced the night away with various partners, not even taking a moment to relax off the dance floor. Late in the evening, when the lights in the ballroom were brought up, her last partner noticed a change in Victoria. To his horror, he found that she had died in his arms while they were dancing.

In light of this tragic event, the hotel reached out to her father, the Louisville judge. That is when the first red flag appeared. This man did not have a daughter named Victoria. No one knew who Victoria actually was. Eventually, her room was entered, and the single trunk she had traveled with was found empty. This woman had no identification and none of the traditional travel items of the time. Her body was held for a week to see if anyone would claim her, but no one did. It was finally decided that she should be buried, and a site was picked out on the hotel grounds, just feet from where she had died. The hotel and its guests held a funeral for the beautiful unknown woman. The mystery of this nameless woman's death haunted the town from that night on.

Years after this tragic event, in 1853, the hotel and its various buildings were sold and became the Western Military Asylum, a type of veterans' home, before the buildings mysteriously burned to the ground one by one, with the final falling in 1885. Another resort opened in 1912, but that too came to an end when the mineral springs dried up in the following years. Around this time in the early 1900s, the story of the dancing woman took a turn. The tragic story and her oddly placed grave started to be associated with another mystery.

Around this time, the first written report of strange occurrences near the hotel appeared. People reported seeing a woman dancing near the resort. Those bold enough to speak to the woman would find that she would indeed answer and ask for directions back to the ballroom she died in. When told the ballroom was gone, the distraught figure would disappear, terrifying unsuspecting bystanders.

After the closing of the hotel and the mysterious fires that destroyed the veteran's home, the city of Harrodsburg decided the location should have a new life and is now home to a park and children's playground. Opening the property to the public has exponentially increased the sightings of the Dancing Lady. Individuals have reported seeing a figure dancing in the park where the hotel once stood. Others have seen a crying woman near the gravesite itself. One eyewitness told *Oxygen* they heard someone say, "It was a mistake. It wasn't supposed to happen," leading some to believe foul play may have been involved in the Dancing Lady's demise. The specter and her appearances kept her mysterious life in the forefront of the mind of the town, and people could not stop trying to figure out just who Victoria Stafford actually was.

In 1938 a local paper, *The Lexington Leader*, reported one man's account of exactly who he thought the Dancing Lady was. The story started with a name: Molly Black Sewell. She was a Tennessee native with a tragic story of her own. Molly was said to have escaped an unhappy marriage and traveled to the resort, where she met an untimely end. This was said to have been confirmed by someone who had met her husband years later. Modern investigations into this account have led some researchers to question its accuracy.

During the pandemic in 2021, another attempt to identify the dancing woman started. A local historian and cold case investigator teamed up to petition the city to exhume the woman's body to see if they could identify her via DNA. A darker theory than her tragic death is that she may have been murdered by the nephew of the owner, Dr. Christopher Columbus Graham, who was reported to have violent outbursts. There is little connecting the two on the night of the Dancing Lady's death, but the nephew was arrested for murder in New Orleans just a few years after he had left his uncle's hotel. In this theory, her dancing death was nothing but a clever cover-up and could explain why she was buried at the hotel as opposed to in a local cemetery. There are other theories, including that she was not traveling alone and that her mysterious travel partner fled after the death, that she could have fallen to a cholera outbreak and her death was covered up, or that the entire story may be nothing but a publicity stunt by the owner of the Graham Springs Hotel, and the coffin would be found to be empty on exhumation.

At this point, there has been no exhumation. The Dancing Lady, Victoria Stafford, Molly Black Sewell, or whatever her name may have been, still lies in her small grave, feet from where she met her tragic end. The explanations of who she may have been in life have changed over the years as new theories have emerged. The one consistent detail is the encounters reported by locals and visitors alike of seeing a dancing figure, a crying woman, or a shadow in the park near the tiny grave

that would draw their attention only to vanish before their eyes. This strange grave and the phantom that accompanies it has kept this unknown woman, her tragic end, and her mysterious life alive in the minds of this small town for well over a century and is driving the next generation to find a name for this nameless soul.

References:

Banim, Julia. "The Mystery of the Dancing Lady." *Unilad*, June 7, 2021. https://www.unilad.co.uk/featured/the-mystery-of-the-dancing-lady.

Bartlett, Marvin. "Unkown Grave in Harrodsburg tied to Ghost Story" Fox Lexington, November   1, 2016. https://foxlexington.com/news/local/unknown-grave-in-harrodsburg-tied-to-ghost-story/

Graham Springs; Harrodsburg Kentucky, Historical Marker erected in 1969, marker number 1297.

Harrodsburg Springs; Harrodsburg Kentucky, Historical Marker erected in 1962, marker number 551.

Holland, Jeffrey Scott. Weird Kentucky: Your Travel Guide to Kentucky's Local Legends and Best Kept Secrets. New York: Sterling Publishing, 2008. Page 205.

Marsh, Jennifer. "Researchers Seek to Exhume Harrodsburg's Dancing Lady." *The Harrodsburg Herald*, March 3, 2021. https://www.harrodsburgherald.com/2021/03/03/researchers-seek-to-exhume-harrodsburgs-dancing-lady/.

Marsh, Jennifer. "Was Harrodsburg's Dancing Lady Murdered?" *The Harrodsburg Herald*, February 3, 2021. https://www.harrodsburgherald.com/2021/02/03/was-the-dancing-lady-murdered/.

Tron, Gina. "Was The Mysterious 'Dancing Lady of Harrodsburg 'Actually Murdered? Sleuths Try To Find Truth Behind Legend." Oxygen True Crime. February 5, 2021.https://www.oxygen.com/crime-news/todd-matthews-and-dr-lynne-smelser-aim-to-identify-kentucky-mystery-woman

Some ghost stories from local ghost tours and locals' stories.

THE CANONICAL LIE

Amanda R Woomer

"I am down on whores, and I shan't quit ripping them till I do get buckled."

-Jack the Ripper
Dear Boss letter
September 25, 1888

TRIGGER WARNING: THIS ARTICLE MENTIONS AND DEPICTS IMAGES OF VIOLENT MURDERS AGAINST WOMEN.

It's said to be "the world's oldest profession." Rudyard Kipling coined this term in only 1898, and yet it has somehow become an accepted historical fact. Prostitution is certainly not the world's oldest profession (surely that title goes to farmers, bakers, tailors, builders, and butchers). Still, it can be argued that it's one of the most important professions, building empires and saving economies. And yet, despite its role throughout history, sex work is a controversial topic… and always has been.

Throughout history, kings and popes were allowed to have their courtesans, while women working in the alleys and out of cribs were controlled by the police, ostracized from society, and targeted by violent and cruel individuals.

Perhaps the most (in)famous attack on prostitutes became headlining news, beginning on August 31, 1888, and continued through the "Autumn of Terror."

The Jack the Ripper murders are seemingly connected to 19th Century prostitution. The area of Whitechapel was part of the slums of East London. At the time, the local police estimated approximately 62 brothels and 1,200 prostitutes living and working in the area. Poverty was widespread, leading many women to try to earn extra money as prostitutes, including all of Jack's victims…

Contemporary 1888 illustration of P.C. Neil discovering the body of Mary Ann Nichols with his lantern.

…At least, that's what we've been taught. It's become an accepted fact that each of Jack the Ripper's victims was a prostitute (perhaps that was why they were each targeted). The "canonical five"—Mary Ann "Polly" Nichols, Annie Chapman, Elizabeth Stride, Catherine Eddowes, and Mary Jane Kelly—were complete unknowns and undesirables when they lived. Yet, they have become celebrities in death. We have very few images of them in life, but the artistic renditions and the horrific photographs of the crime scenes are well-known among dark history nerds, internet sleuths, Ripperologists, and historians worldwide.

We've been told that these women were in the wrong place at the wrong time, no doubt soliciting the wrong man. And yet, only Elizabeth Stride and Mary Jane Kelly worked as prostitutes in Whitechapel. The other three women were homeless (like so many others in Whitechapel) and tried to make a living off of begging or the occasional odd job such as selling flowers, cleaning, and crocheting. And while living with a man or having a child outside of wedlock also earned women the title of "prostitute" in the late 19th Century, for some reason, even in the 21st Century, the label has stuck for Mary Ann "Polly," Annie, and Catherine.

Why does history claim Polly, Annie, and Catherine were prostitutes alongside Elizabeth and Mary Jane? Some historians and Ripperologists believe the word "prostitute" in this sense is used as a way to lessen these women as human beings. By dehumanizing them, both contemporaries and 21st Century historians (and those simply curious about

Annie Chapman on her wedding day, 1869.

Jack the Ripper) can look at the case and the images of the murders without guilt. The word "prostitute" is used as a barrier to protect us from the horrors these women experienced in their final moments, and in so doing, it has rewritten the narrative of not just sex workers throughout the Victorian Era but the lives (and afterlives) of these women as well.

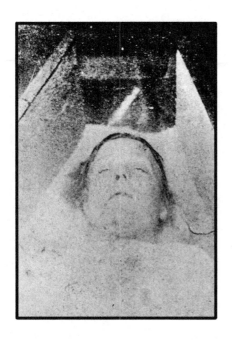

Polly Nichols was a charwoman (part-time cleaner) who was separated from her husband. She had a bit of a criminal record which included drunkenness and disorderly conduct. When her body was found on August 31st, she had bruises on her face, wounds on her throat, her vagina had been stabbed twice, and several cuts along her abdomen forced her bowels to protrude from her body. However, no organs were missing.

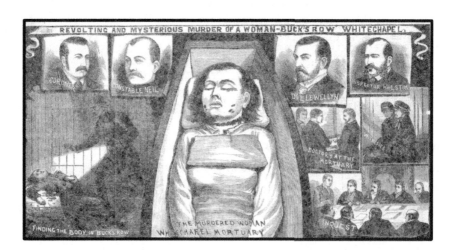

Annie Chapman had amicably separated from her husband in 1884 and became a flower seller and crocheter. She lived with another man who left her in 1886. Annie became depressed and seemingly "lost the will to live." Annie was last seen alive on September 8, 1888 at 5:30am in the presence of her killer. By 6:00am, her body was found with wounds similar to Polly Nichols—two deep wounds across her neck and her abdomen was mutilated.

Elizabeth Stride was born in Sweden, moving to England in 1866. She became a prostitute at a young age and married in 1869. The couple had a tumultuous relationship and after her husband's death, Elizabeth lived with another man as well as in local lodging houses. At 12:35am on September 30th, Elizabeth was seen with a man and by 1:00am, her body was found. Unlike the other canonical victims, Elizabeth only had one cut along her neck that was still bleeding and parts of her body were still warm. This has led many to believe that Jack the Ripper had been interrupted in his grisly plan. She is the first victim of what is known as the "double event."

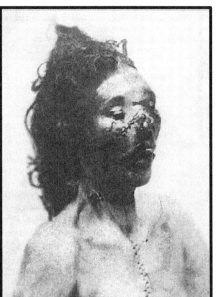

Catherine Eddowes grew up in London, and was sent to the workhouse when she was just 15 years old. Catherine was described as a cheerful woman who liked to sing but had a temper. Catherine had a partner named Thomas Conway (with no evidence of the two ever marrying) and two children but by 1880, she had left them on account of her drinking and her husband's abuse. On September 30th, at 1:44am (less than an hour after Elizabeth Stride was found), Catherine Eddowes' disemboweled body was found. Like all the other women, her throat was slit, and her face was badly beaten with her intestines pulled out and draped over her right shoulder. Her left kidney had also been carefully removed. This led the coroner and others to believe the killer may be a surgeon or a butcher. Several weeks later, part of a human kidney was sent to the police along with the infamous "From Hell" letter. In it, Jack the Ripper claimed the half of the kidney sent to the police belonged to Catherine while he had eaten the other half.

FINDING the MUTILATED BODY IN MITRE SQARE

Registration District			Whitechapel				in the County of Middlesex		
1888.	Death in the Sub-district of		Spitalfields						
No.	When and where died	Name and surname	Sex	Age	Occupation	Cause of death	Signature, description, and residence of informant	When registered	Signature of registrar
326	9th November 1888 13 Miller's Court Christchurch	Marie Jeanette KELLY otherwise DAVIES	Female	about 25 years	Prostitute	Severance of right Carotid artery. Wilful murder against some person or persons unknown. Violent	Certificate received from R Macdonald Coroner for Middlesex Inquest held 12th November 18	Seventeenth November 1888	W. Edwards Registrar

Mary Jane was born in Ireland in c.1863, though not much about her life is known. After her husband died around 1881, Mary Jane began her work as a prostitute, relocating to London in 1884. For a short while, Mary Jane worked at a high-end brothel in the West End of London. Within a year, Mary Jane began drinking heavily and moved to the East Side of London. She lived with several men over the years, eventually settling into 13 Miller's Court with Joseph Barnett. On the night of her murder, Mary Jane was spotted at the Ten Bells Pub and the Horn of Plenty Pub before a neighbor saw her enter her room with a stranger at 11:45pm. Her body would be discovered almost 12 hours later when Mary Jane's landlord came to collect the rent at 10:45am. Finding the door to her room locked, he peered in through the window to discover Mary Jane's mutilated body lying on her bed. Since the murder took place inside and not in public, the killer was able to take his time. Her throat was slit, the skin was removed from her groin and thighs, her organs were removed and scattered throughout the room, both of her breasts were cut off, and her face was beaten beyond recognition. None of her family attended her funeral.

It's been over 130 years since a madman targeted these women, declared "prostitutes" to make the public feel better about the tragedy, and dubbed them the "canonical five." Today, the lives of the canonical five are overshadowed by their gruesome deaths and the infamy of their killer. Whether they were seemingly easy targets, homeless, prostitutes, or simply alone, it's time to remember them for who they truly were:

Mary Ann.

Annie.

Elizabeth.

Catherine.

Mary Jane.

Learn more about the Canonical Five and the history of sex work in Amanda's book, *Harlots & Hauntings*. Available at spookeats.com/shop

References:

Begg, *Jack the Ripper: The Facts*, p. 43

Hume, R. (2020, May 18). Tragic saga of Jack the Ripper's Irish victim, Mary Jane Kelly. *Irish Examiner*. https://www.irishexaminer.com/lifestyle/arid-30960082.html

Inquest testimony of Edward Spooner, quoted in *The Times*, 3 October 1888

Jones, R. (n.d.). *Mary Nichols The First Victim Of Jack The Ripper*. Jack the Ripper 1888. https://www.jack-the-ripper.org/jack-the-ripper-victim-mary-nichols.htm

Lister, K. (2021). *Harlots, Whores & Hackabouts: A History of Sex for Sale*. Thames & Hudson.

Rubenhold, H. (2020). *The Five: The Untold Lives of the Women Killed by Jack the Ripper* (Reprint ed.). Mariner Books.

Rumbelow, D. (2013). *The Complete Jack the Ripper* (Revised, Updated ed.). Virgin Books.

Selwood, D. (2017, August 31). On this day in 1888: Jack the Ripper claims his first victim in the world's most infamous unsolved murder spree. *The Telegraph*. https://www.telegraph.co.uk/news/2017/08/31/day-1888-jack-ripper-claims-first-victim-worlds-infamous-unsolved/

Sheldon, N. (2001). *Annie Chapman: Jack the Ripper Victim, a Short Biography*.

Wescott, T. (n.d.). *Casebook: Jack the Ripper - Old Wounds: Re-examining the Bucks Row Murder*. Casebook: Jack the Ripper. https://www.casebook.org/dissertations/rn-old-wounds.html

Woomer, A.R. & Taylor, T. (2022) *Harlots & Hauntings*. Spook-Eats.

BETWEEN WORLDS:
PREGNANCY AND THE PARANORMAL

Sarah A Peterson-Camacho

My son was born dead.

This is the first time I've written these words, let alone acknowledged their existence.

I was high as a kite for my second Caesarean; my lower half burned that quickly mellowed to numb. But I still knew blue when I saw it—he was the shade of a bruise as it ripens to plum. And then Tim was gone. My husband saw the doctors working on him, but kept silent as I marveled over my lack of gravity—I felt like a floating torso.

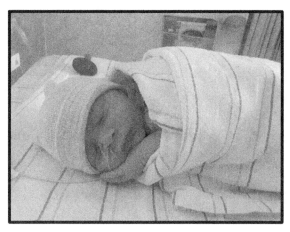

That night I bled out 592 cubic centimeters—20 fluid ounces, or the amount of liquid in a bottle of soda. I could feel the blood soaking through the hospital sheets as the spinal block wore off.

In the buzzing half-dark, it reminded me of ink.

Pregnancy is a portal of sorts. As a soul slips through from the other side, the veil between realms tears open to allow passage—but who knows how long that window remains open? Or if it ever wholly closes?

"Some say the unborn are in a transitional phase between the spirit world and the physical world," so it would make sense that, as the host vessel, an expectant mother—amid the flood of hormones wreaking havoc on her psyche—might morph into an extrasensory powerhouse. Or, at the very least, gain a spiritual awareness as senses are heightened.

> AND IF PREGNANCY IS A KIND OF POSSESSION, AS TWO SOULS INHABIT ONE BODY, THEN CHILDBIRTH IS A KIND OF EXORCISM—BOTH TERRIFYING PROSPECTS THAT HAVE HAUNTED HUMANKIND FOR MILLENNIA, THE THREAT OF DEATH AND DISEASE EVER-PRESENT, EVEN IN THE MODERN ERA.

Threading the online forums and message boards of sites like Café Mom, Baby Center, Net Mums, and What to Expect, stories of pregnancy-related paranormal activity attest to the belief that something supernatural is indeed afoot for some—myself included.

From the explainable (nightmares and sudden chills) to the utterly inexplicable (apparitions and moving objects), eerie similarities abound in these unsettling accounts, particularly in the timing of the ghostly encounters: the hour between 3:00am and 4:00am, known to many as the Witching Hour.

But my brush with the other side—seven months into my pregnancy with Tim—resembled none of these unearthly anecdotes.

On the morning of Tuesday, April 13, 2021, I woke up knowing that one of my mom's estranged friends was dying. It was a woman she had not spoken to in about a decade, who lived across the country on the East Coast. I hadn't thought about her in years, but I dreamed of Margaret Williams that night.

In the dream, I was visiting my parents at my childhood home when their mail arrived. I watched as my mom sliced open a large white envelope and slipped out a funeral program emblazoned with a portrait of Margaret. A hand-written note from Margaret's middle-aged son revealed the news of her passing.

And that was all. I got out of bed and went to work that day, heavily pregnant, filing the dream away in the back of my mind… until my mom called that night.

"Margaret Williams died," she revealed.

"I know," I replied.

"How?" Her tone was incredulous.

"I dreamed about her last night." I filled my mom in on the details of my prophetic dream.

When I first met my son Tim, it was in the NICU, through a maze of tubes and tape. He was born blue and unbreathing, thanks to my preeclampsia and a knotted umbilical cord.

His newborn lungs had been pumped full of oxygen, which blew a hole in one of them, causing a pneumothorax (or collapsed lung). The jaundice was the least of his worries.

As he bathed in the ghost-blue glow of UV rays to treat the jaundice, sporting baby shades, I marveled over the tiny miracle of him—two weeks premature, the hole in his lung slowly mending itself after one hell of a night.

And when we locked eyes for the first time, his gaze was haunted.

> HE HAD SEEN THE OTHER SIDE, BUT HAD MADE IT THROUGH THE PORTAL TO THIS PHYSICAL REALM, SOUL-BRUISED, BUT ALIVE.

Perhaps he had met Margaret Williams—maybe she helped nudge him over the Great Divide into the world of the living.

For that, I am eternally grateful.

References:

Graham, Hilary. "The Social Image of Pregnancy: Pregnancy as Spirit Possession." *The Sociological Review,* May 1, 1976, p. 291.

Sharps, Linda. "9 Spooky, True Stories of Paranormal Experiences During Pregnancy." May 3, 2013. https://cafemom.com/parenting/155096-spooky_true_accounts_of_pregnant.

YULE BETTER WATCH OUT

Brianna Bravoco

I watched the delicate snowflakes fall upon my windowsill, trickling down and dusting the gray and gloomy Berlin streets beneath me. The sweet cinnamon fragrance of freshly brewed *Glühwein* danced through the air. "It's here," I murmured to myself. The magic of December had arrived in Germany, but this Yuletide season had different plans. This Christmas, I was not searching for jolly St. Nicholas. I was looking for his dark shadow—a legend of whispers from the eternally moonlit forests of Bavaria. His name is etched in the silhouettes of darker, ancient Yule monsters. His name is Krampus.

If you travel to the idyllic and frosty regions of Bavaria on the eve of December 5th, you will find a different type of Christmas festivity. A celebration of ghastly nightmares beyond your wildest dreams, this devilish jubilee is *Krampusnacht* (Krampus Night). Krampus is a menacing, demonic, anthropomorphic goat with a crimson, forked tongue and pointed horns. This Yuletide Boogeyman carries a chain with bells that he thrashes about and a bundle of birch sticks meant to swat naughty children. His name originates from the German word *krampen,* meaning "claw."

According to alpine legends, he is the son of Hel, the Norse god of the underworld. Krampus is described as a satyr-like spirit who is the anti-St. Nicholas and determines whether children have been naughty or nice. According to lore, if naughty, one would be lucky enough to receive a beating from the Krampus with his frightening birch twigs. In the worst-case scenarios, he would lead children off a cliff, toss them in a frozen lake, eat them with his pitchfork, or throw them in his sack to be hurled off to the bleak and unforgiving Underworld.

The next day, December 6th, is *Nikolaustag*, or St. Nicholas Day, when children would gingerly look outside their door to see if the shoe they'd left outside the night before contained either presents—a reward for good behavior—or a rod for bad behavior.

Many people celebrate this ancient tradition in present-day Austria, Germany, the Czech Republic, Slovenia, Hungary, and parts of the United States. Schnapps-drunken men dressed as wooden-masked devils take over the dimly lit streets for a *Krampuslauf*—a Krampus Run—where people are chased through the streets by these alcohol-infused Christmas beasts. They shriek like banshees, steal your mittens, they growl like a bear, and whip the ground with their chains and sticks from hell. You can run, but you can't hide. The Krampus is coming for you.

Krampuslauf *in Pörtschach am Wörthersee, Austria, 2012.*
Photo courtesy of Johann Jaritz

No one exactly knows the origin of Krampus, but it is believed to be the remnant of pre-Christian Alpine traditions of heathenry and paganism, originating from Austria, Germany, and the Czech Republic. However, there's very little hard evidence left to prove this theory.

Despite the lack of evidence, Maurice Bruce wrote in *Folklore* in 1958 that:

> *...there seems to be little doubt as to his true identity for, in no other form, is the full regalia of the Horned God of the Witches so well preserved. The birch—apart from its phallic significance—may have a connection with the initiation rites of certain witch-covens; rites which entailed binding and scourging as a form of mock-death. The chains could have been introduced in a Christian attempt to "bind the Devil," but again, they could be a remnant of pagan initiation rites...*

-Maurice Bruce, *Folklore Vol. 69, No. 1,*
March 1958

Other historians said he is derived from the era of the Moorish raids in Europe, where people were kidnapped and sold into slavery. Krampus's menacing presence was suppressed for many years by the Catholic Church. In the 12th and 13th Centuries, the church forbade the raucous celebrations due to its pagan origins and likeness to the devil. Again, in the 1940s, fascists in World War II Europe found Krampus despicable because it was considered a creation of the Social Democrats. The Krampus has been repeatedly banned

Photo courtesy of Matthais Kabel

and denounced by child psychologists since 1953 for being psychologically "scarring and traumatizing." Back in 2006, concerned parents and Austrian child psychologist Max Friedrich spoke out against the demon's violent influence, as well as so-called childhood "Krampus trauma." But despite all this bad publicity, Krampus remains a tenacious spirit who can't seem to be expunged by religion or government.

Amongst all the debauchery and adrenaline-fueled celebrations, I had to wonder: Were these Austrian psychologists on to something? These liquor-soaked Krampuses often turn violent and beat up boys or use this night to rob unsuspecting victims. In 2014, a woman was beaten by a drunken Krampus in Salzburg and had to be hospitalized.

> I BEGAN TO BELIEVE THAT SOMETHING MORE SINISTER HAPPENS TO THE MEN WHEN THEY ARE INTERTWINED WITH THE KRAMPUS ROLE—SOMETHING DANGEROUS.

Like they are in a possessed trance, the Krampus masks seem to uncover what is normally suppressed. As stated by author Holly Müller in her novel, *My Own Dear Brother*:

> *Usual boundaries fall away; forbidden urges are given outlet. Can a simple mask transform us; change us? Or does it simply permit the demon already within to emerge?*

Peter Wiesflecker, an Austrian historian of culture and customs, warns the cult of the Krampus has evolved into a mass spectacle, and the traditional festival is becoming a real danger.

"If a large group of young men in masks roamed the streets on any other night of the year, the police would be called out in an instant," said Wiesflecker. "In an anonymous collective, we are always more likely to overstep our boundaries."

Krampus is gaining ever-increasing admiration amongst pop culture and mainstream media. Could it be because he challenges everything the early Christians venerated as Holy? Or is it because of our subconscious desire to let our inhibitions down during these nocturnal Bacchanalias? It would appear that on these gloomy winter nights, the Krampus is not the creature we should fear, for he is just a mirror of our dark depths of human nature staring back at us.

References:

Bruce, Maurice, Folklore Vol. 69, No. 1, March , 1958.

Conny Waters, Krampus Celebrations Are Becoming Dangerous –
Historian Warns, December, 2019.

Muller, Holly, My Own Dear Brother, Bloomsbury USA, 2016

Ridenour, Al, The Krampus and the Old Dark Christmas: Roots and Rebirth
of the Old Folkloric Devil, Feral House, 2016

The Local Austria, Woman beaten by man dressed at Krampus, December
2014

THE SÉANCE :
RECREATING CLASSIC VICTORIAN SPIRIT PHOTOGRAPHS

Selina Mayer and
Rebecca Pointeau

PHOTOGRAPHER :

Selina Mayer (https://www.selinamayer.com/)

PHOTOGRAPHER'S ASSISTANT :

Tristan Nieto (http://tristannieto.com/index.html)

SETTING :

Victorian Séance Room, Museum of the Home, Shoreditch, London
(https://www.museumofthehome.org.uk/)

MODELS :

Rébecca Pointeau (Instagram @vulgar_superstitions)
Dr. Romany Reagan (https://blackthornandstone.com/)
Andrew Burgess (https://www.sableindustries.org/)

CAN YOU DESCRIBE THE CAMERA YOU USED AND THE PROCESS OF USING THE CAMERA AS ORIGINALLY DESIGNED?

Selina: The camera used is a Victorian Half-Plate camera, originally used for the wet-plate and dry-plate processes. Wet plates are sheets of glass coated with light-sensitive emulsion immediately before the photograph is taken, and must be developed within 10 minutes (i.e., while the plate is still "wet"). Dry plates (which we used for this series) use a slightly different light sensitive emulsion that can be coated and dried in advance and then processed later. Dry plates allowed for the mass production of plates for photography for the first time, so they opened up photography as an activity to a much broader range of people as you no longer needed as much specialist knowledge.

In order to take a photograph using a plate camera, you must frame and focus your image first, using the ground glass at the back of the camera, which has an upside-down and reflected image from the lens. Then (in darkness), you load a light-sensitive plate into a darkslide, a device that slides into the back of the camera and protects the plate from light until you're ready to take the photograph. At the time, photographic lenses and shutters were separate and most shutters from the period are difficult to find fully functioning because of their mechanical nature, so when I use this camera, I use it without a shutter, taking the photograph by removing the lens cap and manually counting the seconds of exposure before replacing the lens cap.

In what way was this standard process altered to create the spirit photography images?

Selina: I still used this process when making the spirit photos, with a few early special effects techniques thrown in. Most of the transparent, ghostly figures were created using multiple exposures (i.e., shooting several images onto the same plate), usually blacking out the area during the second and/or third exposures, so you don't expose the background twice. But I also made use of moving objects during the long exposures, using a fault in one of the darkslides to create floating beams of light, or using very thin thread to make an object "float." I then made prints in the darkroom and used further manipulation techniques (known as "dodging and burning") to make some parts of the final images lighter or darker.

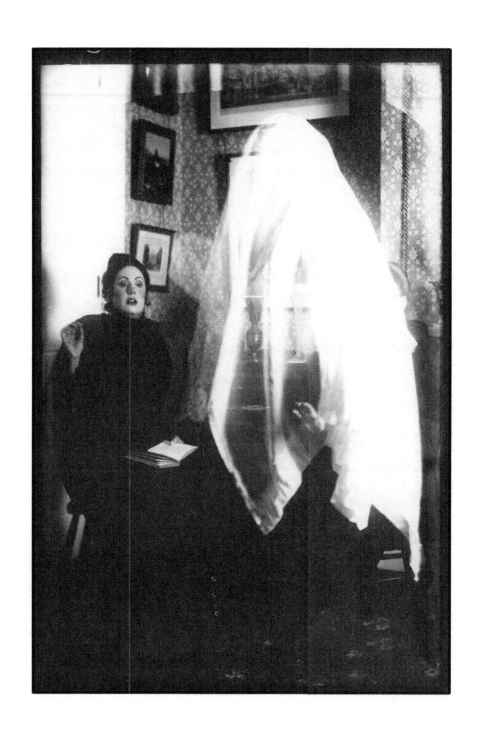

WERE THERE ANY SURPRISING OR UNEXPECTED MOMENTS DURING THIS SPIRIT PHOTOGRAPHY PROJECT?

Selina: I think the entire process was something of a jump into the unknown! Using analog processes means that you can't see the result immediately, which is challenging in and of itself, but then throw in the fact that we were in a location I'd never been in before, using manual techniques that can't fully be predicted, meant that every plate was a leap of faith. One of the delights of working with such old, analog processes and techniques, however, is that it allows for "happy accidents" to occur—the funny quirks of the processes that you didn't anticipate but end up falling in love with—which definitely happened during this project and just made the final images more special because of their uniqueness.

Trauma Response and the Paranormal

Jessica Krutell

Trigger Warning: This article mentions the Covid-19 pandemic.

I have always been a firm believer in the paranormal. From a very early age, my family encouraged the idea of an afterlife, with my mother and grandma often sharing their family ghost stories with me. My grandma had witnessed everything from UFOs to full-body apparitions. I grew up watching *Ghost Hunters* with them and loved the idea of becoming a paranormal investigator myself. Eventually, I was able to make those dreams come true when I formed Mystic Mitten Paranormal Group. My mom was our biggest fan, never missing a livestream or library presentation. Occasionally "Mystic Mom" would even participate in various ghost hunts. Her familiarization with using our equipment led her to understand life after death better.

The Beginning of the End

After becoming ill in April of 2021, my mom and I went together to get tested for COVID-19. When the rapid test came back positive, we both laughed because we did not believe it could possibly be anything more than Midwestern seasonal allergies. Little did we know how severe things would get.

Unbeknownst to me, this would be the last bit of time I spent with her. I will never forget telling her how much I loved her as she drove off in her blue Ford Flex.

I started to recover, whereas she showed no signs of improvement. I went back to work, and she went to the hospital after much convincing from my brother. My mom was only 62 years young, and besides needing a knee replacement, she was in good health.

Days Before Her Passing

Like many others during the pandemic, my husband worked from home. Leaning more towards skeptic beliefs, he tolerated the altar I set up in the study with photos and items belonging to loved ones who have passed on. My grandma's trinkets and mementos from her funeral have a place of honor. Shortly after my mom was admitted to the hospital, my husband heard a knock coming from the wall behind the altar. It was one of several signs that my grandma was nearby. I realize now that the knock he heard was my late family arriving to bring my mother home.

My husband was not the only person to hear death knock. A few nights later, I fell asleep on the couch while watching TV. I woke up to a very loud and sudden knocking at the side door. Thinking it might be a burglar, I lay there in fear until I realized the motion lights by the side entrance had not been activated. How could someone be knocking and not trip the sensor? Days later, my mom's health quickly declined.

In a matter of hours, the severity of the infection had increased—always one step forward and two steps back. She was put on a ventilator, and her kidneys started to fail. I reached out to individuals from as many origins and belief systems as I could conjure to ask for prayers. I figured if multiple religions and higher powers were called upon, we would stand a better chance of witnessing a miracle.

At this point, I began to contact extended family to let them know the seriousness of the situation. I reached out to my mother's cousin, with whom she shared a special friendship. She and I had similar beliefs regarding life after death. A student of mediumship and Reiki, she told me that a friend of their family, another medium, had recently contacted her. Having no prior knowledge of my mother's rapidly declining health, the medium reached out to ask why my late grandmother was "here." My mother's mother returned and revealed herself to this close family friend. This was further proof that our family would meet us again.

THE NIGHT OF HER PASSING

We were granted permission to visit her in the ICU. Strapped up in hazmat gear, we took turns visiting our mother one last time. I had recently studied aura reading which taught me ways to transfer energy. I sat over my mom and created balls of pure white light, pushing them into her body with hopes it would be enough to get her through the evening. Maybe this would be enough to help her kidneys recover and reverse her organs from shutting down.

My family was later gathered outside in the waiting room, where my father, brothers, and our spouses sat silently as tears fell from our faces. We were the only ones in the room with a handwashing station to prepare for entering and exiting the ICU. Suddenly the motion-activated paper towel dispenser went off on its own. No one was near it as we were all sitting on the opposite side of the room. I looked at my dad, who gave me a "did you see that?" look as he stated that it was Mom waving "goodbye."

I wasn't willing to accept that it was her, so I said, "No, it's just Grandma saying hello!" I tried to convince myself that my grandma was there to tell her to return to her body. Visitation hours had ended, and we all needed to return home for the longest and most gut-wrenching night of our lives.

I decided to spend the night with my dad and my youngest brother. I lay in my bed, in the home I grew up—where my mom used to tuck me in and kiss me goodnight. We lay there staring blankly at the ceiling, dreading any phone calls, willing the phone not to ring. I finally drifted off to sleep.

A few hours later, I was jolted out of sleep. It felt as if I was just suddenly shocked with a defibrillator. An immense amount of electricity bolted through my body from my fingers to the tips of my toes. The house phone rang before I could process what had just occurred. I jumped out of bed to find my father crying on the line with the doctors. He was crying; things did not look good. Her oxygen levels were declining. Decisions had to be made. Did we want them to resuscitate her? Yes! My mom is a fighter! We would not give up on her.

We woke up that morning to rush to the hospital, hoping to catch her right as visitation hours began. We arrived moments after they pronounced her dead. Later I realized that the moment I was shocked awake was when her spirit left her body. Our spirits don't always go at the moment our hearts stop. She returned that energy to me, knowing I needed it.

THE NIGHT BEFORE THE FUNERAL

I am now the matriarch, not by choice, but as the eldest sibling and the only female next of kin, I was left with making most of the funerary decisions. Orchestrating her funeral arrangements was mentally and physically exhausting. Like my mom had done for me so many times, I picked the outfit she would wear, her nail polish, and her lip color. My mom was a stickler about having good hair days. Since that was my sister-in-law's expertise, I enlisted her help, for which I will be forever grateful. As the day ended, everything was planned as well as possible. The photo boards complete, and the readings selected. It was finally time to lay down and try to get some sleep.

Later, I found myself standing in my parents' living room with my mom beside me. She talked about her passing and told me to take care of myself. I woke up with a heavy heart, bracing myself against what I knew would be some of the worst days of my life. We held the funeral during a spike of COVID-19, in the middle of a global pandemic, not being able to hug or be held by our extended family and friends. There was a limited headcount and strict rules we had to follow. When they say those who suffered a loss from COVID-19 are unlike any other loss, I can truly attest to that.

> ## GRIEF DOES NOT UNDERSTAND RESTRICTIONS.

NIGHTS WENT BY

My dog and my mom were best friends. After her passing, my dog would lay in her crate for hours. No amount of coaxing could bring her out. You could tell she was experiencing her own sadness and loss. One morning around 2:30am, my dog started acting irrationally. She looked up at the corners of the ceiling, saw something I could not, and then proceeded downstairs. I was not sleeping much anyway, so I tiptoed after her. I found her walking around the basement sniffing, and every so often, she would pinpoint a specific area and wag her tail. Mom used to play hide and seek with my dog and would often hide in the basement and then whistle for my dog to find her. My mom was here and was playing hide and seek! Of course, it happened at this crazy hour—she was quite the night owl! I set up my REM Pod on the kitchen table and tried to do a question-and-answer session to no avail. My dog went back downstairs, and I followed again. This time, I had a device set up to detect energy fields and temperature changes. The REM Pod upstairs would ring as my dog would narrow into a spot and begin wagging her tail. For several nights there was similar activity, although it rarely occurs now.

THE DREAMS CONTINUE

I was in my parents' bathroom, watching as my mom pulled new clothes out of a dress bag hung on the curtain rod. The sun shimmered through the window on her "forever outfit" she showed me. An outfit very much her style, but I had never seen it before. The top was a light purple with a distressed wash and a pair of comfortable and soft denim shorts. She was happy and excited to show off her new clothes. Shortly thereafter, I woke up.

A couple of nights later, I had another dream. We sat in our old maroon Toyota Camry outside an unfamiliar apartment complex. She was in the passenger seat holding our late Pomeranian. Our dog pranced onto the center console. I ran my hand through her fur. It was still fuzzy, and she was full of energy. My mom was an avid dog lover. I find peace in knowing they were reunited at the Rainbow Bridge.

OUR RELATIONSHIPS GO ON

Some might ask, "Why doesn't my loved one visit me?" You have to understand that my relationship with my mother was unlike most others. She was my biggest supporter and my paranormal group's biggest fan. She loved watching ghost shows with me and even went on multiple investigations. She was familiar with our ghost hunting equipment, allowing her to have a different understanding than most regarding communication in the afterlife. She knows this is what I would want. Although you might truly think you need a visitation or an experience, your loved one might see that you are not ready. A visit could do more emotional harm than good. Only they truly know.

Our loved ones continue to be around us daily through small miracles. I recommend having an open mind and looking for signs all around you. These signs show your loved one is near as long as your mind is open and willing to accept them. Pay attention to your dreams! I am no expert (as one cannot truly be an expert in this field). Still, I believe the difference between dreams and dream visitations is that dreams seem to be in real-time, whereas in visitations, time is slowed down, and every detail is remembered. Often in visitation dreams, the deceased acknowledge their death, the detail is clearer, finer, and time feels like it is stuck in silly putty. It has been just over a year, and the dream visits happen less and less often.

Throughout multiple support groups on Facebook, I have started to see a trend that I am not alone. Many others who also lost a loved one to COVID-19 are experiencing similar activity. In situations like these, many of us were unable to say goodbye. Often these deaths were untimely and left a residual trauma that those affected will have to carry for the rest of their lives. My family was fortunate enough to be able to visit my mother the night before her passing and the morning shortly after we lost her. However, many others were not so lucky.

> THIS LEADS ME TO BELIEVE THAT THESE SPIRITS ARE WILLING TO WORK EXTRA HARD TO VISIT US AND GIVE A MORE FORMAL GOODBYE.

I hope that this story brings you some comfort and peace of mind. If there is anything I can promise you, it is that when we die in this world, it is not the end. I have experienced far too much that you simply cannot convince me otherwise.

IN LOVING MEMORY OF CAROLYN M. KRUTELL
"MYSTIC MOM"

Are You a Witch? Are You a Fairy? Are You the Wife of Michael Cleary?

Monique Rose

A children's rhyme echoes through schoolyards as young girls skip rope and chant in unison, their tiny voices hitting each line in monotone-fashion with every turn of the rope:

> "Are you a witch? Are you a fairy? Are you the wife of Michael Cleary?"

The sound of this verse during schoolyard play may seem haunting enough, but who *was* the wife of Michael Cleary? And why has she been immortalized in this way?

Born in Tipperary, Ireland, in 1869, Bridget Boland was a woman ahead of her time. She grew up in an era where superstition, mysticism, and what is now considered folklore frequently ruled over reason. However, that foundational belief system was considered heresy as the rapid spread of Christianity replaced it. Though one could argue this was only replacing one form of superstition with another (in terms of religious beliefs), the way of the church meant sophistication and progress. Subscribing to Irish folk beliefs, on the other hand, would earn someone the reputation of being uncivilized and even barbaric. Bridget's young adulthood in Ireland unfolded as many were caught between ancient ways and new advancements in politics, medicine, and science. Ireland was in the midst of a new era, but it wasn't all excitement and growth. There were times of internal conflict and confusion, as even those in Bridget's own household were at odds with themselves, often struggling to renounce the old ways to embrace the new.

Bridget herself was something of a strong spirit, distinctly beautiful, and a wonderful mix of these opposing worlds. She spent some time daydreaming and visiting nearby fairy rings, balancing herself with hard work. She was very successful in helping to provide for herself and her husband, Michael. Michael was a tradesman, and though Bridget's beauty and fierce independence (along with their lack of children) occasionally made them the  subject of village gossip, the couple was held in good social standing. The young Mrs. Cleary was a skilled dressmaker. She loved creating fashion with vibrant, modern design.

Bridget was known to be daring and unabashed when it came to her manner, her style, and her entrepreneurship. This young, lively self-starter developed her craft into a successful business, all while running the household, raising hens, and selling eggs to nearby villagers. She was independent and forward-thinking. The qualities Bridget possessed were rare in 19th Century Ireland and virtually unheard of in women. As Bridget became more successful and surer of herself, her husband Michael grew suspicious that something was not quite right with his bride of seven years.

It is rumored that a minor domestic dispute broke out when Michael caught a glimpse of Bridget daringly donning red undergarments and black stockings beneath her frock. He was furious that his wife would have the audacity to be so brazen, even in private.

Bridget gently scoffed at her husband and stood her ground. She assured Michael that she was the same woman he had married. She gently reminded him that he had fallen in love with her strength of spirit. From there, Michael grew increasingly paranoid over his wife's brash behavior, though none of the things that worried Michael would be considered grounds for concern today.

It was early March in 1895 when Michel's unease began to boil over, and things would start to go horribly wrong for Bridget Cleary.

Though the winter months were coming to a close and spring was on the horizon, evidence of snow remained on the ground in Tipperary. Bridget made her way on foot to deliver eggs in a nearby village. On her way to Kylenagranagh, she passed a rath, or ring fort.

These stone ruins are ancient remnants of medieval dwellings and fortresses. The structures, also known as fairy rings, are studded throughout Ireland, marked by a circular stone formation. These ancient stones often look as if they have spontaneously risen ever so slightly from the emerald-covered earth—somehow a doorway to another time or place. Commonly believed to serve as dwellings for fairies, these ring forts were widely considered dangerous gateways to the fairy world. Bridget was familiar with stories of the fae, and though most people were warned to stay away from these ring forts for fear of being captured by fairies, Bridget was known to be drawn to them.

In Irish lore, fairies are mischievous and often feared. Culturally, the fae were depicted as shapeshifters. Fairies frequently sought trouble and lived to wreak havoc in the human realm. Many illnesses and misfortunes were blamed on the fairies. There existed a strong, widely accepted belief that fairies were able to abduct people from this world and drag them through a fairy ring. When fairies capture a person, they are replaced in this realm by an imposter called a changeling.

These beliefs were far from Bridget's mind as she walked home from Kylenagranagh. She tried to hurry along—the sun had been shining, but the air was sharp and frigid. The frostiness stung wherever her skin was exposed. Bridget pushed on, clutching tightly to her scarf as the coldness whipped her face. By the time she made it to her own doorstep, her boots and stockings had been soaked through by the half-melted, snow-smattered earth. The cold had chilled her to the core. Hours by the fire were no match for this, and Bridget's condition worsened overnight.

By morning, Bridget was burning with fever, suffering a headache, and came down with a persistent cough. She was extremely lethargic, and her usual vibrant spark had been considerably dimmed. While her cousin, Johanna, suggested Michael call on the doctor, Michael's wheels had been spinning entirely over another train of thought. A doctor was summoned nonetheless, though Michael maintained a skeptical, watchful eye over Bridget's condition. She had, after all, been acting more defiant in recent weeks, and she *had* been through Kylenagranagh the day before. Michel knew what existed on the path to that village and knew that his dear "Bridgie" was known to visit these fairy rings. Had she tempted fate one too many times?

It took the doctor several days to call on the Cleary house. He was only there a short time before diagnosing Bridget with acute bronchitis, in addition to "nervous excitement." He noted that Bridget's condition was nothing of great concern. The bronchitis was straightforward, and he chalked the nervous excitement (known today as anxiety) up to Bridget's delicate state of being a woman. He gave Bridget some medicine to help ease her through the worst of it before instructing friends and family to allow her to rest. He saw no reason Bridget wouldn't make a full and swift recovery.

> **HIS VISIT UNCOVERED NO EVIDENCE THAT BRIDGET WOULD BE DEAD IN LESS THAN NINE DAYS.**

Though family and neighbors surrounded her, poor Bridget did not alert any of her loved ones or visitors of what had begun to unfold privately in the Cleary home. Her husband Michael had all but decided that Bridget was no longer herself. He was convinced that the changeling who replaced her needed to be expelled as soon as possible.

Due to the persistence of her illness, the family sent for a priest. Father Ryan promptly visited the home. Much like the doctor, the priest surmised that Bridget would be well enough in no time. Michael watched from nearby as she received communion. Still too sick to get out of bed, she choked down the dry communion offering. Her husband stared at her with eagle-eyed focus, watching for the slightest slip up to reveal what he already believed to be the truth.

After the room cleared and Father Ryan had taken his leave, Michael, maintaining outward composure, slowly took hold of a red-hot iron poker from the fire. He casually sauntered over to Bridget's bedside. Despondent, Michael slowly lifted the glowing end of the metal rod and steadily drew it closer and closer until it was only inches from her face. The pulsing heat radiated from the iron, making the short journey to her delicate skin.

"Are you Bridget Cleary, in the name of God?" Michael screamed at her menacingly.

Cousin Johanna listened from the next room. Frightened and broken down, Bridget was hardly able to summon an answer. "I… am Bridget Cleary… Your wife!" she finally mustered.

Her wide, tired eyes were filled with fear, confusion, and heartbreak. Michael loomed over Bridget a few moments longer, holding the smoldering iron dangerously close to her skin, determined to break her. Exhausted, Bridget slipped out of consciousness, and Michael stepped back. Dissatisfied by the doctor and believing that the changeling had fooled Father Ryan, Michael returned to the main room of the home, where the family was still gathered. He sat down and instructed them to send for Dennis Ganey.

Ganey was a fairy doctor: an expert in the fae folk and how to dispel them. He entered the Cleary home, reinforcing every fear that had consumed Michael over the last several days. Along with his support of Michael's claims, Ganey brought an arsenal of herbs and rituals to aid in removing the changeling from the home. According to Ganey, they had only nine days from the moment of the abduction to expel the creature, or Bridget would be forever lost to the fairy realm.

The following days were spent aggressively questioning Bridget. She was force-fed herbs and threatened with fire. Many visitors would come and go over the next few days, but none of them would speak against the abusive treatment of Bridget as she recovered from her illness. Few friends and family members followed Michael down his spiral into madness but all were complacent in their silence.

The ninth day arrived, and though Bridget was slowly regaining her strength, Michael continued to read into every action… every *inaction*. He was on a mission, but whether that mission was to rescue his wife remained to be seen. "I'm right here, Michael. It's me! It's Bridget," she pleaded as he shouted profanities and dowsed her in holy water.

She began to recover enough that she could think more clearly. Her sharp mind was steadily returning, and Bridget saw that pleading with Michael was not getting her anywhere. She convinced Michael that she had gone to the fairy ring in Kylenagranagh, and she was taken by the fairies for a moment, only to be returned home on the first day. She was back now, and she was Bridget Cleary! This revelation, she thought, would be more than enough for Michael. The married couple stared at one another. After a long, intense pause, her gamble seemed to have paid off. Michael slowly reached up and cut her bindings. Her arms collapsed to her sides. Michael called for cousin Johanna to enter the room and help Bridget into her clothes. Bridget slowly stood and dressed layer by layer. Johanna helped keep her steady while Michael's glare continued to burn into her every move.

The three entered the next room, where friends and family were gathered. Elated at the sight of Bridget, they rejoiced and helped her to the table. They offered Bridget some tea. Michael loomed in the shadows, pacing the edge of the room. He did not take his eyes off the group as he slowly positioned himself and locked the front door. Cousin Johanna, her mother, and her brothers exchanged nervous looks. Michael set three pieces of bread down before Bridget. She was expected to eat all three dry crusts of bread before he would allow her even one sip of tea.

Under a heightened level of distress, she struggled to swallow the bread. Watching carefully, Michael readied his vile of "Seven Sister's Kill or Cure." Supplied by Dennis Ganey, this foul concoction of herbs and urine is used when ridding the home of a changeling, though it must be saved for the ninth and final day. As the name suggests, the potency of this mixture would either kill the subject or cure them.

"What's this about, Michael?" Bridget's father, Pat Boland, interjected, noting the drastic change in atmosphere. Michael lunged toward Bridget, throwing her to the ground at the opening of the stone hearth. His knee pressed against her chest as he clutched her jaw in his powerful grip. He forced the final piece of bread into her mouth and began to pour the kill or cure down her throat.

"This is not my wife, and you will soon see her go up the chimney!" He tore at her clothing to reveal her black stockings. No wife of his wore black stockings. He was determined this meant the changeling never left. Onlookers stood frozen in horror as Michael reached for a nearby canister. He proceeded to pour lamp oil over Bridget, who lay still, nearly lifeless at his feet. The group pleaded with Michael to unlock the door and regain some level of reason. Screams of protest broke out as Michael set Bridget alight. Her chemise violently erupted into flames.

A heavy layer of smoke enveloped the room. The bystanders watched helplessly for a moment before clamoring to unlock the door. Johanna felt the pure terror, heartbreak, and intense stench of burning flesh overwhelm her senses. Her cousin's body burned not three feet away from where she stood. The effervescent light of a woman they all called Bridget was gone. They all knew it was too late. Michael, however, was still desperate. There he waited for Bridget to return from the fairy realm on a white horse. This is, after all, what the folklore promised. Three days he waited, in vain... Bridget Cleary died on March 15, 1895.

The hearth where Bridget Cleary was burned alive.

The badly damaged body of 26-year-old Bridget Cleary was buried in a nearby shallow grave. A black hood covered her once beautiful face, now charred.

Michael Cleary was prosecuted for the murder of his wife in what would be known as "The Fairy Trial." Bridget's murder was used as political propaganda to perpetuate the idea that the belief in Irish folk practices was uncivilized and often a dangerous way to live. Johanna Burke testified in court about the circumstances culminating in the death of her cousin. Ultimately, eight people were convicted for their roles in the death of Bridget Cleary—a woman so bravely bold that, according to her husband, could only have meant one thing: she had been taken by the fairies. Whether or not she was a witch, a fairy, or the fiercely free-thinking wife of Michael Cleary, Bridget was taken from the human realm far too soon.

Today, when little girls chant the jump rope rhyme, let them invoke Bridget's spirit—a strong woman who came before, unafraid to be bold, independent, and dangerous to those who should ever attempt their subjugation.

"I SEE DEAD PEOPLE:"
CHILDREN AND THE PARANORMAL

Nicole Long

"I see dead people."

This chilling line from *The Sixth Sense* is the eeriest and most quoted from the modern-day classic thriller about a young boy who helps Earth-bound spirits complete their unfinished business before moving on to the next realm.

The idea of the psychic child isn't new, dating back to at least the 17th Century. William Parry, a 12-year-old who claimed to be possessed, caused mass hysteria, and thousands flocked to his Staffordshire village. Even though claims of this possession were faked, it brought attention that children could potentially see or hear things that aren't there. The sheer number of kids seeing ghosts (no matter how improbable or unprovable) has forced some scientists to take notice of the phenomenon.

But the question is: why do children see ghosts more than adults? Is it their innocence and openness to the idea that there is something more out there?

As children, we had imaginary friends—there would be tea parties or games of hide and seek with someone who wasn't there.

Research shows that between one-third and two-thirds of children have imaginary companions. A psychologist at Durham University who investigates the phenomenon of hallucinations said, "Not too long ago, imaginary friends were considered a precursor to mental illness; now we know they're a positive sign of healthy child development."

Many researchers explain there could be more to this than simply a child's imagination. Blair Robertson, a psychic medium, states, "I believe that we all have the ability to experience spirits. Young children don't necessarily have an increased ability, just innocence that allows them to experience spirits without bias or filters." In this case, we have to look at the innocence of children and the idea that this innocence can lead to their perception of spirits.

As we grow into adults, our perception of reality changes because we learn about the world around us. We learn from the "real" and expand our minds into the reality that is seen. Children don't have a sense of reality, yet as their minds are growing and developing, they think the little girl in the corner is their best friend because that is what they see. The naivety of children allows them to see objects and things that may not be there. Their brains are functioning on a level of understanding and forming new objects that have never been seen before. This can cause the openness and vulnerability needed for spirits to communicate with children. There is also a popular belief that children can lead us to the other realm because they still have a foot in both our world and the spirit world.

One mother recounted that her three-year-old twins once sat down for a pretend tea party with a woman named Magdalina. No big deal, right? Well, Magdalina happened to be the name of their late great-grandmother, who died two days before their birth.

Another story includes a woman named Rachael Rogers, who was putting her four-year-old son, Thomas, to bed when he began talking about a "man in his room." Rachael was a single mom—she and Thomas lived alone—and as far as she could see, they were the only two people present. But her son was insistent, pointing at the empty spot beside her, saying, "He's there, standing next to you. Look!"

These are just two examples of countless stories where children see the other side without knowing just what they are seeing.

No matter the cues we get from children about the paranormal, there is something to be said: their vulnerability can create a vision that most adults will never inhabit. Should we be scared when a child introduces us to an imaginary friend or makes claims that there is a figure in the corner of the room? Many psychologists advise parents not to panic if their child starts sharing stories about encountering a ghost. Communication with the child is vital. In these circumstances, taking the child's lead and asking direct questions is of the utmost importance: Where did you see it? What does it look like? What do you know about it? How do you feel about it?

It is important to remember that if the child does not fear the apparition, you shouldn't either.

Let their intuition do its thing.

References:

https://blairrobertson.com
https://www.dailymail.co.uk/home/you/article-7891245/What-kids-ghosts-Anna-Moore-hears-tales-send-shivers-spine.html
https://www.newfolks.com/

A Filmic Cyber Haunting

Kachine Moore

In the past decade, screencast or desktop cinema has increasingly harnessed the disquietude surrounding the collective unconscious understanding of our diminished free will within the digital age. In a world that longs for re-enchantment, creators and filmmakers endeavor to formulate different and post-cinematic ways to captivate their audiences. Modern exhibition of cinema can easily fit in your pocket and travel with you, and the collective absorption of moving images in everyday life is commonplace. Nevertheless, "newness" is a fluid concept, and finding something new within the old is imperative.

British Zoom horror film *The Host* (2020), directed by Rob Savage, not only reflects our current condition and exhibition interface during the global COVID-19 pandemic but activates a new narrative avenue for horror cinema as spectral hauntings now can travel virtually through cyberspace.

Premiering on the online horror streaming service Shudder, *The Host* (2020) opens with an actual Zoom meeting homepage, similar to the Snapchat opening in thriller *Sickhouse* (2016) and Skype and Facebook horrors *Unfriended* (2014) and its bleak sequel *Unfriended: Dark Web* (2018). Yet, this particular screen's interface is pure 2020. Zoom grew exponentially during the unprecedented global health crisis/COVID-19 pandemic. Individuals and companies overnight needed to create a remote work environment via online video conferencing, helping to save more than 2 million jobs in the United States alone. Zoom has become as valuable for companies and institutions as the cell phone.

In this film, a group of women meets up on Zoom from the safety of their respective homes to partake in a virtual séance led by a spirit medium. Out of respect for quarantine, one girl even bangs on the window of her friend's apartment to be let out of the program's waiting room so that they do not come in contact with each other.

Since complicated staging and visual depth of field are complex and as rudimentary as a camera's laptop, the footage is limited to the bust-like portrait mode of the actors, and a few shots of the actors walking around their homes with the computer. The group jokes about typical Zoom issues they have with multiple cameras having feedback; they even mention trials and tribulations of lockdown, like staying indoors, living with family, and moving in with new partners for the first time. They play around with each other before the séance starts using standard Zoom funny face filters and video wallpapers. This opening sets up the possibilities and online geography of the Zoom space as now wallpapers can double as special effects. Non-diegetic effects such as a scrolling participants page were also used for the end credits.

As spectators of the film, we are at the same vantage and point of view as the actors/characters. It is an exhibition of each individual through a computer screen. The interface allows more of a connection to the events taking place. As they see, we see, almost as if they can see us, the audience, leaving a sense of foreboding and anxiety. This exhibition style and plot device act like a subliminal mutual feedback network.

The virtual séance begins as the moderator or spirit medium explains to the group about the astral plane having no language or restrictions because, through the internet, disembodied consciousness will do whatever it can to communicate, manipulate something, and turn anything into what makes sense to us—the potential of this concept for narrative is captivating.

The medium mentions trigger objects, common in paranormal investigation, which are any personal objects with which the spirit or whomever they would like to speak to have a connection; she also plays ritual tones to create a link to the spirit realm. They light candles in their own respective houses to guide focus as a beacon the spirits can come towards.

> THE INTERTWINING OF THE TECHNOLOGICAL LANDSCAPE AND PHYSICAL OR CORPOREAL OBJECTS CONNECT BOTH REALMS OF CONSCIOUSNESS IN A WAY FILMMAKING HAS NOT UTILIZED BEFORE.

Cyberspace, governed by its binary structure, creates a sense of anonymity with potential for play and creative parallels to metaphysical cultures. In its most basic form, virtual reality is a reproduction or digital version of our experience of reality. Real effects are produced by something that is not fully actual, so cyberspace becomes entwined with the discourse of the transcendence of the body. This mind/body dualism is fundamentally Platonic and Cartesian metaphysics.

> LIKE GHOSTS, FLESH HUMANS USING THE INTERNET CAN ACT AS A SPIRIT, AS CYBERSPACE REMOVES THE CORPOREAL BODY AND FREES THEM OF THEIR EARTHLY LIMITATIONS.

During an in-person séance or spell casting, there is a connection between participants, the creation of a circle, or the holding of hands, which creates a protective barrier and connection to the conscious realm. But with an online séance that does not exist and the possibility of being less protected within the unknown foreshadows the terror to come.

The girls participating in the séance begin to experience physical activity. One girl feels a light touch on her shoulder, they hear knocks and thuds, and they see little lights flashing in the backgrounds of their screens. Each participant acts as if they are highly affected emotionally by the experience. Then, in the plot's rising action, one girl tells a tall tale about a dead classmate trying to reach out to her during this session. Suddenly, the medium's Wi-Fi goes out and gets ejected from the chat. This deception creates a strange relationship to and unease concerning the Zoom, as we now, as spectators, are unsure of what is real in the story's context and what is being made up by the characters.

Then the real hauntings begin but within their own IRL spaces. Unable to rejoin the Zoom call, the spirit medium speaks on the phone to the girls throughout their experience and tells them that they have summoned a "false" spirit by faking a ghost story on the web. Within the sacred space, accidentally manifesting this false entity, and by tricking her friends, the spirit wears a mask on the web, almost signifying regions of the dark web or an incognito mode browser. At one point, a character takes a polaroid photograph of a spectral figure or ghost—this relates ambiguity of the online space and seizes to make the spectator understand through an analog form.

The Zoom add-on functions begin to be used as plot devices and act as goggles to perceive the spirit entity, creating suspense. A virtual background cuts in and out, showing and then hiding a murder, and the goofy filters aim to expose ghosts as they float on invisible faces. Tropes of Zoom, like the extension of time from 45 minutes of the free capability to paid unlimited, become part of the horror. At one point, one girl goes to find her neighbor IRL, who was attacked by the entity on screen, and she climbs through an actual window with her Zoom window open on her mobile phone. When another guest of the séance joins late, they are immediately affected by the haunting as if logging on is enough to make a spirit angry. However, even after their friends die and have been attacked violently by an entity, they still do an elbow-shake greeting in fear of contracting COVID.

Historically, horror cinema has always found common ground by situating itself to exploit fears about the mysteries of the unknown relating to technology. *Blair Witch Project* (1999), the original found-footage horror, and *Paranormal Activity* (2008), with its six additional sequels and a seventh coming out next year, utilize a surveillance style of capturing hauntings. Along with the plethora of amoral AI aiming to end civilization, ghosts or spirits of humans and demons using analog technology to terrorize have had a nascent effect in the genre. *Ringu* (1998), the Japanese horror film, attached a vengeful spirit to a VHS tape that, when watched, harassed its victims by phone and then literally comes out of the TV to kill them. In *Buffy, the Vampire Slayer*'s season one episode, *I Robot, You Jane* (1997), the high school's computer science teacher is a self-proclaimed Technopagan and member of a local cyber coven. As she scans and uploads a grimoire to the web, a trapped medieval demon is unleashed into cyberspace, electrocuting its victims. When the demon is first uploaded, it types out "Where am I?" on the computer screen; this question demands we reimagine the topography of virtual space itself. Like in Plato's *Allegory of the Cave*, the virtual is the outside world or a higher level of understanding.

The virtual possibilities of paranormal engagement through cyberspace create more options for plot-driven action. With this platform, filmmakers can transcend the notion of the material and the material body, as cyberspace has infinite potential. Hauntings—material and immaterial—can now occur with any internet connection/5G network and pass from character to character instantly, with pop-ups, phishing emails, and texts. Humans can act as ghosts on the internet because they are free from their corporeal bodies and limitations. Still, the possibilities multiply in combination with the non-living spirits or entities on the web. The invention of Deep Fake and Hologram technology, and its modern use on stage to present dead performers, is also a hackable point of entry for spirits. Cyber or online manifestations, such as Captcha scrying or auto-generated data output for fortune-telling, can be considered part of this universe.

Cinema can be considered a liminal space, an anti-structure of existential revolt against structure that seeks catharsis from the immunization of life and experience that structure imposes. Liminality is a realm between one place and the next, part of a tripartite system as the threshold illustrating ambiguity and transition. It functions similarly to cyberspace, as the web is a place of "becoming" without actually "being." It is a place of possible trajectories where we can posit our individuality and permanence within the world.

This film is at the precipice for a new type of interaction and engagement a filmmaker can have with its audience. By utilizing the desktop, our portal to cyberspace—a parallel universe, a realm of pure information—a spectator can move from the objective world of the material to the subjective and symbolic land of consciousness. Logging into the web and accessing technology is like traveling from every day to a post-organic universe. *The Host*'s camera work and desktop interface, reflecting the 2020 pandemic time capsule of Zoom exchange, utilize the horror genre to explore the philosophical concepts concerning mind/body dualism. The film uses those theories as a plateau to delve into a new environment of the paranormal and spiritual hauntings kindred to the narrative structure of gnosis, transcending the limits of the material.

References:

Ittelson, Brendan "A Story of Agility and Innovation: Findings from the Impact of Video Communications During COVID-19 Report" 2021, blog.zoom https://blog.zoom.us/findings-from-the-impact-of-video-communications-during-covid-19- report/

Willis, Holly "Live Cinema" Fast Forward: The Future(s) of the Cinematic Arts, Columbia University Press

Brians, Ella, "The 'Virtual' Body and the Strange Persistence of the Flesh: Deleuze, Cyberspace and the Posthuman" Deleuze and the Body, Edinburgh University Press

Benedikt, Michael Cyberspace: First Steps, 1992, The MIT Press, Cambridge Massachusetts

The Importance and Meaning of Ghost Marriages in Modern Spirit Work

Bianca Ascher

When actively working with spirits, you must be open to all kinds of methods to give them the peace they are searching for—even unusual ones.

In my 28 years of experience working with spirits as a healer, I've gathered and discovered quite a few of these very uncommon and possibly even unknown methods. One important aspect of being a healer is working with the spirits on why they are still in our world and how you can help them move on.

One of the solutions to the problems experienced by spirits is a "ghost marriage," something I have experienced myself. It is believed that some spirits are stuck in the world of the living because they were never married in life. They still wish to find a partner and fulfill their deepest desire to get married… even after they've died. While working with these spirits, this has put me into some interesting situations.

I started researching why a spirit's need to be married was strong enough to keep them here. It turns out it's not as unusual as I thought. In several cultures around the world (especially historically speaking), it is vital to get married, so you do not have to venture into the afterlife alone. Even more surprising: a person can still get married after they have passed away. These solutions were called ghost marriages and took place thousands of years ago in Asia.

Today, singles might use a dating app to find their perfect match, but in Ancient China, there was a custom that would ensure a dead loved one who hadn't yet married would not remain single in the afterlife.

Ghost marriages have been held for nearly 3,000 years. The "bride's" family would pay a dowry to the "groom's" family. Both age and family background were important, so many times, families would enlist the help of a matchmaker. The wedding ceremony consisted of a funeral plaque for the bride and groom and a banquet for the family. The bride's bones would then be dug up and placed in the groom's grave. The macabre tradition of ghost marriages was originally strictly for the dead. However, recently, at least one living person has chosen to marry a corpse... and it seems as if a business is growing around ghost marriages even in the 21st Century.

According to Huang Jingchun of Shanghai University, the price of a bride's bones (especially if they're young) has significantly risen over the years. A family could sell their daughter's bones for 30,000 to 100,000 yuan. The sale of corpses was banned in 2006, but grave robbers today still make a business out of buying and selling the remains of a potential ghost bride. Some believe that women have been murdered for their bones as well.

Today, this ritual is still practiced in northern and central China in provinces such as Shanxi, Shaanxi, and Henan, as well as among Chinese communities throughout South East Asia. These ghost marriages are believed to appease the dead and help them enter the afterlife.

While this may seem like a controversial topic to some, it seemed like the solution I was looking for.

My first "customer" was a 39-year-old male spirit named David. He had died in a tragic car accident in 1956 and was never married— he was too shy to find a girlfriend back in the day. But he was willing to work with me to bring himself some peace.

And so, after creating a very personal ritual together, we were married. And after just seven months, he was finally ready to leave this world and went happily into the light.

It was a fascinating time and taught me so much about other cultures' ways of helping spirits who are stuck here. It also helped me think of new ways to solve problems with my spiritual clients—I would never have thought of marrying a spirit myself.

Working with spirits is so much more than simply communication. If you are willing to learn from them, it can open so many doors (some doors you didn't even realize were there!).

If you still think ghost marriages are odd, it is legal to marry your partner who has already passed away in France. The French government changed this law in 1959, and it's usually a ceremony that helps secure your financial status.

Perhaps ghost marriages aren't so strange after all…

THE PHENOMENON

Susan A Jacobucci

Derby Wharf, located in Salem, Massachusetts, once served as a trade gateway to the colonial world. Unlike today's open recreational landscape, the wharf was once filled with multi-family tenements, warehouses, and merchant shops. The wharf—including the Derby Street neighborhood—was formerly described as "alive with bustle and excitement" and as a place where "…swarthy sailors were grouped at the corners, or sat smoking before the doors of their boarding-houses, their ears adorned with gold rings, and their hands and wrists profusely illustrated with uncouth designs in India ink."

The Derby Wharf landscape is emotionally charged with the memory of people's daily lives. The land embodies their sweat and tears, their happiness and joy, and is otherwise a "basic unit of lived experience." Economic statuses for merchants and shopkeepers at the height of colonial trade transitioned from "poverty to grandeur." Exotic commodities poured into the wharf from points around the world, fueling this transformation. The lives of warehouse workers, sailors, and crew were entangled with long hours of labor. Sailors and crew were separated from their loved ones and away from home for long periods—many lives filled with intense despair, never reunited with their family, and others became hopelessly lost at sea. Can events from this emotionally charged history also be embedded in the land?

I became acquainted with Derby Wharf in the early 1980s, shortly after I moved to Derby Street. I frequented the site, enjoyed walking along the wharf that extends into Salem Harbor, and relaxed on the grassy lawn adjacent to it. I had only known Derby Wharf to be what it was to me at the time: a recreational landscape devoid of building structures. I knew little of the wharf's history until, one day, I seemingly collided with its maritime past.

One would think everything associated with that day in late May of 1983 would be deeply etched into my memory like a riverbed into bedrock. However, only the approximate time of day, the month, the year, and of course, what I saw remains with me. Perhaps the mundane particulars of the event (or as I like to call it: "the phenomenon") have escaped my mind simply because I subconsciously did not want to associate with it. Nevertheless, some mornings I get a strange déjà vu feeling that is hard to explain. On those mornings, I think about the phenomenon like a vivid flashback culminating in a fantastical instant replay of the experience.

The phenomenon took place mid-morning. I remember feeling unusually rested that day before I went for a walk. There was still a numbing chill in the air even though the sun shone bright and strong. I didn't get too far. I had traveled along the sidewalk of Derby Street approximately one block when I looked up at the Salem Custom House and curiously noticed the front door propped wide open.

I thought it was strange how I was drawn to the Custom House that morning. Even though I  walked past the stately three-story, red-bricked, whitish-beige trimmed, black shuttered American Federalist style building daily, I was never really interested in visiting it until that day. I usually focused my attention away from it to across the street to Derby Wharf and the surrounding harbor.

The Custom House is an impressive building with its eight cream-colored columns in front, four on either side of a central door, with a large gilded eagle perched prominently in front of an octagonal cupola, between two tall bricked chimneys on top of a hip roof. I quickly crossed Derby Street and traversed the uneven brick sidewalk.

I climbed wide, light gray granite steps leading up to the front door of the Custom House. I was energized with a spring in each step as I jogged up the remaining stairs to the entrance located on the second floor of the building. I turned and glanced back at Derby Wharf. In 1983, the wharf was devoid of the docked *Friendship of Salem* and all building structures and improvements that are there today, except for the Derby Wharf Light Station situated at the end of the wharf adjacent to the harbor. Derby Wharf was quiet that day, with the occasional visitor walking about the park. I turned back towards the Custom House, approached the open front door, and crossed the threshold of the building.

A docent, faceless, middle-aged man appeared out of nowhere and stopped me short in my tracks before vehemently instructing me not to touch anything and to be careful while I viewed the exhibits. As quickly as the docent appeared, he disappeared, leaving me alone. I walked about the second floor of the building, starting to my right, wooden floors creaked with almost every other step I took. I viewed displays containing artifacts, tools used to measure, and scales used to weigh goods shipped to Salem from around the colonial world. Exhibit captions described some of the exotic goods brought into port, such as textiles, silks, cinnamon, fine ceramics, and ivory, that were processed through the Custom House. I continued looking about the second floor, almost completing a full circle. To my right, I approached Nathanial Hawthorne's office.

I was surprised to discover Hawthorne once worked as a Customs Officer—a Surveyor for the City of Salem from 1846 to 1849. I entered Hawthorne's former office and touched something! I traced my fingers through the dust that collected on top of what was supposedly his desk and was immediately drawn towards one of the large arched windows trimmed in white overlooking Derby Wharf. As I approached the window next to it, tacked on the wall was a page from the introduction of Hawthorne's novel, *The Scarlet Letter*. The page described Hawthorne's office from when he worked there and his view of the wharf and surrounding merchant establishments. The complete introductory chapter shares the author's thoughts and feelings about the Custom House building and his opinions of the glorious past and current decaying state of Derby Wharf when he was employed there. The arched window afforded Hawthorne a bird's eye view of the wharf.

I gazed through the window and caught a glimpse of a surprisingly active vista—however, the sun was no longer shining, and large charcoal clouds had rolled in. Several three-masted ships with raised sails were docked along the wharf. Seagulls circled the top of the masts of the tall ships, which were slipping behind a developing smoky fog that quickly obscured them. A couple of weathered wooden one- and two-story structures stood adjacent to one another near the center of the wharf; teams of workers dressed in dark colors—navy blues and dark browns—appeared to be hauling wooden barrels and pallets from the ships toward the buildings. A white horse pulling a wooden wagon came out of a shroud of mist and approached the Custom House.

I couldn't believe what I was seeing. Derby Wharf was alive! I felt spooked. Goosebumps formed on my arms. I closed my eyes and pressed them tightly before popping them open wide with fright.

The sun was shining brightly once again. The ships, workers, buildings, and horse-drawn wagon were all gone. The wharf was desolate like it was when I arrived at the Custom House. Only several seagulls remained, circling high above the abandoned wharf. One seagull dropped a mussel shell to shatter upon the hard ground. I closed my eyes and whispered, "What did I just see?"

I slowly opened my eyes. Derby Wharf was, as I saw it last, desolate and quiet. I was overwhelmed by a sudden urge to flee the Custom House, but not out of fear. I felt the need to race out and examine Derby Wharf. I quickly made my way to the front door of the Custom House and ran down the granite steps. I stood on the brick sidewalk and stared directly across the street at Derby Wharf. The wharf remained quiet. There was no visible trace of the momentarily lively scene. My bruised emotions were raw while I tried to comprehend what I had seen. Even though the experience lasted seconds at best, it seemed like I had witnessed a scene from the past.

For whatever reason, that day, I could peer into a slice of the wharf's history to an earlier time when Derby Wharf was the center of a bustling seafaring merchant community.

While I have always been a fan of the paranormal and the unexplained, I also consider myself a skeptic with an open mind. Educated and formerly employed as an archaeologist and a science instructor for a Veteran's Upward Bound program, I subscribe to the scientific method. I have always believed there has to be an explanation with tangible factors for creating the Derby Street phenomenon. When I experienced the phenomenon, I was a teenager attending college without prior knowledge of the wharf's earlier history. I had always known Derby Wharf as a parklike piece of land without building structures. How would I know the wharf was once a bustling seaport, and why would I see it that way?

There are two identifiable parts to the phenomenon, the observer and the observed event. How credible of an observer was I? Perhaps the phenomenon can be explained through a dream or, in this case, a daydream. The phenomenon, like most dreams, possessed features that transcended the waking reality of space and time and meshed elements of the past and present together. If the phenomenon were my daydream or, as Guiley describes, an "experience in another reality," the phenomenon was an encounter I had in waking reality. Nevertheless, if the phenomenon were a product of my daydream, it was a very vivid, convincing reverie that took on a life of its own devoid of me.

> AFTER ALL, I OBSERVED THE PHENOMENON AND DID NOT PARTICIPATE IN IT.

Maybe the phenomenon was created out of my imagination. Hawthorne's convincing description of the wharf and his sentiments towards its once prosperous past struck a note within me and served as fuel transporting me to another time? While I am the first to admit my vivid imagination, I have never experienced a vision. Could my well-being that day have assisted in the creation of the phenomenon? Is it possible the phenomenon was a product of a delusion, a hallucination, or was brought upon by my own confusion? Kalweit describes experiments in sensory deprivation where subjects are "submerged into an ocean of hallucinations displaying a whole phalanx of magical and paranormal sensations" in a short period. Could the Custom House have served as some sort of a sensory deprivation tank and I the unwitting subject? I consider this explanation unlikely. I distinctly remember feeling unusually well-rested that day, full of energy, my mind alert, otherwise, in a state least likely to come under the influence of misperception.

I sought to revisit the Custom House to see if the phenomenon could be replicated. The examination of the Custom House, for now, will remain as a future investigation. The building was not open to the public initially due to the COVID-19 Pandemic and now to extensive building renovations and repairs.

Happenings like the phenomenon have also been attributed to past life surfaced memories or past life recalls. Even though, as a child, upon hearing the mere mention of Salem, Massachusetts, I grew excited, and finally, in my teen years attending college in Salem, I am confident I cannot attribute the phenomenon to a memory from a past life. I did not feel personally connected to what I saw. I was detached from the phenomenon and simply a spectator, nothing more than perhaps being in the right place at the right moment.

Could the phenomenon be explained as a time-slip or a residual haunting? Humans have been fascinated with time travel with time-slips recorded throughout history. A time-slip can be described as a supernatural experience in which a person, or group of people, can seemingly traverse time either into history or to a future destination by undetermined measures. Did I observe a slip in time where I could transcend the concept of time as it is linearly defined and witness a prior event?

Through my research, I reviewed descriptions of several time-slip accounts. The accounts had no explanation for how or why these events occurred except the premise that time is fluid rather than fixed and is not linear as we have been conditioned to experience time, thus possibly creating "parallel realities we can visit if we shift our consciousness."

One popular time-slip occurred in 1901 when two friends, one an English academic, Charlotte Moberly, and Eleanor Jourdain, both seemingly credible witnesses, visited Versailles. They left the *Grand Trianon* and entered the garden, *Petit Trianon*, and as they walked about, they recalled experiencing "an extraordinary depression" as they seemingly interacted with men and women who were dressed in period clothing. The two friends initially concluded that *Petit Trianon* was haunted. They later returned to the garden and again experienced what they described as a "heavy, eerie feeling" and stated that perhaps they witnessed distant figures from the past, while Charlotte remembered hearing music playing in the distance.

The pair believed they experienced time travel. After going public with their experiences, their research was condemned for being "unreliable and amateurish." Charlotte later wrote a book entitled, *An Adventure with Appendix and Maps,* which described their visits to Versailles and included evidence to substantiate their time travel claim. Some of their evidence included Charlotte's recollection of clothing she remembered seeing one of the women wearing, "light-coloured skirt, white fichu, and straw hat," which compared exactly to a particular ensemble worn by Marie Antoinette as described by her dressmaker. Upon Charlotte and Eleanor's return to Versailles, they couldn't find a section of woods they had wandered through or other features they witnessed, such as a meadow, a bridge, and a chapel. Nevertheless, their research discovered historical accounts and maps of the site, which documented some of the features they recalled seeing.

Was there evidence from my witnessed phenomenon to substantiate time travel? At the time of my experience, I did not know the history of Derby Wharf nor what kind of ships docked there. I recalled seeing vessels with three masts. Through my later research, I learned that ships known as Salem East Indianmen were "durable, full-bottomed, three-masted ships developed to meet the needs of post-independence commerce." I recalled the coloring of the clothing worn by the workmen. Through my research, I learned trousers "would frequently be white or natural canvases if made of duck, or the grays, blues, and browns of work clothes of the period," which fits my description of the dark-colored clothing. Finally, I remembered seeing one- and two-story wooden buildings near the center of Derby Wharf. I learned at one time, there were as many as 15 three-story wooden warehouses and numerous merchant shops situated along Derby Wharf.

Interestingly after Charlotte and Eleanor shared their experiences in Versailles, other visitors reported similar occurrences. The Society for Psychical Research investigated their experiences. In 1982, one of their members conjectured the events Charlotte and Eleanor outlined "fit a pattern of an 'aimless haunting' that is a haunting not associated with disturbing and shocking happenings and suggested the area acquired emotional power because its inhabitants of the time somehow sensed that their era was nearing an end." Guiley argues the reported sightings are time-slips rather than residual energies since the witnessed men and women wearing period clothing "were not superimposed on the present world."

Witnessed "images, sounds, and apparitions that do not interact directly with people" are examples of residual hauntings. I have spoken with people who have seen residual hauntings, including Mary Lee Trettenero. She refers to residual hauntings as "place memory" and defines them as "energetic residue caused by intense events and emotions, usually from important events" such as battlefields. Hill reports that residual hauntings can be explained by the Stone Tape Theory, which rationalizes that energy from a traumatic event is trapped within the environment from which the event occurred, such as in the bedrock below a location or building materials of a house that is known to be haunted. Residual hauntings have no interaction with the observer and are akin to a recording replayed on a loop. However, what triggers the replay of the recording, such as "the right weather conditions, the witness's energy or sensitivity, or some type of energy release," is unclear.

Was my experienced phenomenon a time-slip or a residual haunting? The phenomenon shared characteristics with other time-slips. Many time-slip subjects reported experiencing intense feelings during the event, such as depression or, in my case, a strong, well-rested feeling followed by an extreme sense of disbelief and awe. Another common characteristic would be that once the time-slip begins, the subjects, myself included, were isolated from their current time period.

The phenomenon, for me, was not transparent or superimposed onto the present world. Instead, every aspect of it belonged to a time from the past except for the location, which connected the past to the present. While the phenomenon obviously occurred at the same place—Derby Wharf—the wharf appeared differently. Like some time-slip experiences, I, too, recalled strands of evidence from the past unknown to me or the observer at the time that matched historical accounts. Many time-slip subjects also report missing gaps of time. I did not experience such a time gap. What I observed also shared characteristics of a residual haunting. The event was nonreactive in nature and observed from a distance. However, the evidence of the phenomenon more closely matched the features of a time-slip because the event wasn't superimposed on the wharf as it currently is but the whole nature of the wharf converted to an earlier time.

Salem's gateway to the world was Derby Wharf, where people became wealthy and worked long hours while others lost their lives. The economy of Salem (and, at times, the nation) depended on the activities that occurred on Derby Wharf. Given the long history of the wharf, the energy of the past could be embedded in the fabric of its geology. This energy could impact the present in certain conditions. More research is necessary to explore whether or not time-slips and residual hauntings occur on Derby Wharf.

The phenomenon that I experienced remains a mystery for now.

References:

Bhattacharjee, Souvik. *Science Behind Paranormal Activities* in International Journal of New Technology and Research (IJNTR) ISSN: 2454-4116, Vol.-3, Issue-3, March 2017, Pgs. 108-112.

Braschler, Von. *Time Shifts: Experiences of Slipping into the Past and Future*. Rochester, Vermont, Destiny Books, 2021.

Casey, Edward S. "Place in Landscape Archaeology: A Western Philosophical Prelude," in *Handbook of Landscape Archaeology*, Bruno Davis and Julian Thomas, Editors, World Archaeological Congress Research Handbooks in Archaeology. Walnut Creek, California, Left Coast Press Inc.

Davies, Paul. *About Time: Einstein's Unfinished Revolution*. A Touchstone Book, Simon & Schuster, New York, NY, 1995.

Ellis, Melissa Martin. *The Everything Ghost Hunting Book: Tips, Tools, and Techniques for Exploring the Supernatural World, 2nd Edition*. Adams Media, An Imprint of Simon & Schuster, Inc., Avon, Massachusetts 2014.

Farnsworth, Cheri. *Haunted Massachusetts: Ghosts and Strange Phenomena of the Bay State*. Guilford, Connecticut, 2020.

Fletcher, Katherine. *Time Slips: Real Stories of Time Travel*. Monee, IL, May 01, 2021.

Guiley, Rosemary Ellen. *Dreamwork for the Soul*. New York, New York, The Berkley Publishing Group, a member of Penguin Putnam Inc., 1998.

Hawthorne, Nathaniel. *The Scarlet Letter: A Romance*. United States, H. Altemus Company, 1892.

Hill, Sharon. *Spooky Rocks* from Skeptical Briefs, Vol. 27.3, January 29, 2018.

Kalweit, Holger. *Dreamtime & Inner Space: The World of the Shaman*. Boston, Massachusetts, Shambhala Publications, Inc., 1984.

McClelland, Norman C. *Encyclopedia of Reincarnation and Karma*. Ukraine, McFarland, Incorporated, Publishers, 2010.

Paine, Ralph Delahaye. *The Ships and Sailors of Old Salem, Massachusetts*. United States, Heritage Books, 2007, accessed through: https://www.google.com/books/edition/The_Ships_and_Sailors_of_Old _Salem_Massa/7xbvj9PDGMsC?hl=en&gbpv=1&dq=Paine,+Ralph+D elahaye.+The+Ships+and+Sailors+of+Old+Salem,+Massachusetts.+Un ited+States,+Heritage+Books,+2007.&pg=PA344&printsec=frontcover

Putnam, Eleanor. *Old Salem*, Edited by Arlo Bates, Cambridge, Massachusetts, Houghton, Mifflin and Company, The Riverside Press, 1886, accessed through: https://www.google.com/books/edition/Old_Salem/KLB4AAAAMAAJ ?hl=en&gbpv=1&dq=Old+Salem+Eleanor+Putnam&printsec=frontcov er

Trettenero, MaryLee. *We're Still Here: The Secret World of Bunker Hill's Historical Spirits*. United States, Happy Otter Press, 2015.

Websites:

https://7gables.org/history/nathaniel-hawthorne/ Nathaniel Hawthorne.

https://ia600303.us.archive.org/15/items/adventurewithapp00mobe/adventu rewithapp00mobe.pdf, *An Adventure with Appendix and Maps*, Moberly, Charlotte Anne Elizabeth, MACMILLAN and Co., Limited, St. Martins Street, London, 1913, Digitized by the Internet Archive in 2010 with Funding from University of Toronto.

https://www.npr.org/2011/10/31/141868232/paranormal-technology-gadgets-for-ghost-tracking Beenish, Ahmed, *Paranormal Technology: Gadgets for Ghost-Tracking*, NPR October 31, 2011, 2.00 PM ET

https://www.nps.gov/places/derby-wharf.htm   Last updated November 7, 2021.

http://npshistory.com/brochures/sama/1982.pdf Salem Maritime Brochure, National Historic Site, Massachusetts.

http://npshistory.com/publications/sama/hfs-derby-wharf-warehouses.pdf , *Salem Maritime Derby Wharf Warehouses, National Historic Site / Massachusetts, Historic Furnishings Study*, Salem Maritime National Historic Site by Charles W. Snell, Denver Service Center, Historic Preservation Team, National Park Service, United States Department of the Interior, Denver, Colorado, November 1974.

http://npshistory.com/publications/sama/index.htm Salem Maritime National Historic Site Massachusetts, *"To the Farthest Port of the Rich East"*.

http://npshistory.com/publications/sama/newsletter/v3n2.pdf *Pickled Fish and Salted Provisions Historical Musings from Salem Maritime NHS, Seaman's Clothing in Friendship's Era*, National Park Service, U.S. Department of the Interior, Salem Maritime National Historic Site, Salem, Massachusetts, Volume III, number 2, March 2002.

https://www.historybythesea.com/a-mystery-on-derby-wharf-rediscovering *History by the Sea, Rediscovering the Lost Buildings of Polish Salem, Salem, MA, USA*, By Jen Ratliff for use by Salem Maritime National Historic Site, Overseen by Emily A. Murphy, Ph.D.

https://www.nytimes.com/2021/11/16/magazine/time-slips-time-travel.html The New York Times Magazine, Elvin, Lucie, *How I Became Obsessed with Accidental Time Travel*, Published Nov. 16, 2021 Updated Nov. 17, 2021.

https://www.salem.org/blog/celebrating-200-years-of-salems-custom-house/

https://www.techeblog.com/5-bizarre-time-slip-cases-where-people-mightve-actually-time-traveled/ *5 Bizarre Time Slip Cases Where People Might've Actually Time Traveled*, TECHEBLOG, December 18, 2013.

Kali, Chaos, and Chainmail:
How I built a Business with Unintentional Magick

Vanessa Walilko

I often do magick without realizing it. I have a sneaking suspicion this is a result of the hyperfocus and dopamine-chasing of ADHD, which propels me with fanatical tenacity to go after what I want and get what I want. This unintentional ritual work is beneficial in chaos magick. Peter Carroll in *Liber Null* says that successful chaotic workings require disconnecting from a "lust for results." Once the hyperfocus of the ritual is done, you shouldn't dwell on the outcome. Assume that chaos will provide for you.

When I started my jewelry business over a decade ago, I wasn't thinking in magickal terms. I just knew that the only thing I wanted to do in the world was make things for a living, and I was willing to do whatever it took to make that happen.

Looking back on that first year, I believe I engaged in a year-long magickal working to build a business for myself. One of the tricks of chaos magick to help train your monkey mind is to create a mantra for the result you're looking for. I wrote on a piece of paper, "Aluminum Chainmail Jewelry Queen," sealed it in an envelope, and then promptly lost it in my massive hoard of notes accumulated over the years. This was my magickal formula for what I wanted to be.

> IT WAS VAGUE ENOUGH TO ALLOW FOR THE UNIVERSE TO MANIFEST THE BEST POSSIBLE RESULTS.

The magickal formula was written, but I needed to figure out the ritual actions to help bring this idea into reality. Before I struck out on my own, I worked for two jewelry designers and learned multiple tricks for building a creative reputation. In that first year of my business, I entered every competition for jewelry or wearable art that I could find. I submitted pieces for group exhibitions, high-end craft fairs, and publications. I applied to teach chainmail at well-attended conventions and submitted projects to various crafts magazines.

Initially, I felt a tremendous amount of anxiety sending out all of these applications. But I just sent so many out that I couldn't keep track of them all. I couldn't stay attached to outcomes because I was always doing the next thing.

And the whole time, along with my name, I submitted applications with my business name: Kali Butterfly. This was my magickal name, even if I didn't realize it at the time. Kali is the Hindu goddess of death, destruction, and time. Kali is also one of the 17 names of Lilith, another of my personal goddesses. Vanessa is a genus name for certain butterfly species, hence the name's second part. The butterfly is also a scientific symbol for chaos with the butterfly effect— sensitive dependence on initial conditions. And what is chaos magick if not making subtle changes in your life initially that lead to significant changes down the road?

And if we want to talk about changes, I made them happen. Despite graduating undergrad with a degree in sociology and no creative connections, I built a name for myself and my business. I exhibited at some of the best art fairs in the country and published multiple jewelry projects in various magazines. I placed or won numerous competitions. I made a living off of selling jewelry for years.

I believe this is partly because Kali Butterfly became more than just a business name. The name itself is an invocation of two goddesses and the element of chaos. The more that name was published along with my work, the more it was associated with not just chainmail jewelry but also elaborate wearable art pieces. And aside from just the glamor magick of fashion, Kali Butterfly was a symbol of pursuing creative dreams despite all social pressures. My friends, students, and customers all saw what I was doing and were inspired. They all believed in me and my business, and all of that energy coalesced into something much greater than I could have imagined.

Joseph Chilton Pearce writes in *The Crack in the Cosmic Egg* that fanatical devotion to an idea brings about its realization. This idea is a bit at odds with chaos magick's focus on not desiring a particular result, but I believe there's a way to reconcile the two. My sense of magick is very broad—I think everyone is capable of doing magick, and I also believe that magick suffuses every aspect of existence.

> I THINK EVERY INTENTIONAL ACTION IS A RITUAL.

Making jewelry itself was a repeated ritual action in support of keeping my business alive. You don't need to cast a circle or light incense to do powerful magick. You just have to keep showing up.

A desire for results can be limiting, but I believe desire in the service of desire itself is very powerful. So many spiritual traditions see the body as a source of suffering and sin, and I think that's a toxic belief that keeps many of us from ever chasing the joy we deserve.

> WE ARE MAGICK. AND WE USE OUR BODIES TO PLAY WITH THE UNIVERSE IN ORDER TO MAKE INCREDIBLE THINGS HAPPEN.

We can visualize what we think will bring fulfillment, but no intellectual idea can capture the pure power of visceral emotion.

While I agree with Carroll that cultivating an intellectual detachment from results will produce more effective magick, I also think that bodied desire is incredibly powerful magick. The mantra— *aluminum chainmail jewelry queen*—evoked the emotional fulfillment of being known and respected for my creative work and making a living off it. I didn't have any idea what the specifics of that would look like, but I chased desire, and I achieved things I could never have imagined on my own.

Asking ourselves who we want to be and what emotional reality we want to experience—those questions can start the subtle alchemy of reconnecting us to the magick that is a part of all existence.

Introductory Scrying Techniques

Jamie Michelle Waggoner

What is Scrying?

Whether you realize it or not, you're probably already familiar with scrying. From the infamous incantation, "Mirror, Mirror on the wall, who's the fairest of them all?" spoken by the evil queen in *Snow White*, to Galadriel's magical mirror pool that shows the past, present, and future in *Lord of the Rings*, to the popular (and creepy!) "Bloody Mary" sleepover game, scrying continues to be part of our collective psyche.

The word "scrying" comes from the Old English word *descry*, which means "to make out dimly" or "to reveal." Outside of its appearances in literature, film, and pop culture, the practice of scrying is still utilized around the world as a way to access information through extra-sensory perception (beyond the five waking senses). Its basic techniques are simple and accessible to everyone.

Scrying tends to be a highly individualized insight practice, similar to such activities as dreaming, meditation, and trance journey. Almost all of the images, symbols, and/or impressions you may experience through scrying are unique to the symbolic language of your own unconscious mind. Practicing scrying over time, and recording your observations, can help you draw connections between this symbolic language and ordinary reality.

PREPARATION FOR SCRYING

Choosing Your Medium

Scrying uses a medium to help focus our inner attention: common mediums are water, mirrors, crystals, and fire. Different mediums have different energetic personalities. For example, scrying into water feels "watery" energetically—water represents the realm of emotion, memory, love, receptivity, relationships, dreams, connections, and the suit of Cups in the Tarot. By contrast, scrying into a flame feels "fiery" energetically—fire represents the realm of passion, action, adventure, optimism, energy, combativeness, and the suit of Wands in the Tarot.

The Crystal Ball *by John William Waterhouse, 1902.*

Choose a medium that speaks to your personality, imagination, and intuition, or play with all of them if you like! Your natural preferences will show themselves in time. It will be easier to concentrate and receive meaningful insights using your "preferred" medium.

Later in this essay, we'll discuss specific techniques for working with three types of scrying mediums: water, mirrors, and flame.

Purifying and Consecrating Your Tools

Choosing a scrying medium will determine what type of tools you will acquire. For water scrying, you will need a bowl or small cauldron. For mirror scrying, you will need to buy or make a black mirror. For fire scrying, you will need a fireproof dish and candles, a fireplace, or an outdoor fire pit.

Purifying your tools removes any residual energies, and clears the way for you to build a relationship with them. There are several methods of purification. You can give your tools a "moon bath" by placing objects in full moonlight overnight. Some people like to immerse their tools in salt water to purify them, but be wary: salt can be corrosive to many materials (especially metals). Others use sound vibrations, such as ringing bells or chimes, over and around their tools. My favorite method of purification (for myself and my tools) is smoke cleansing: placing dried herbs directly on a hot charcoal and wafting the object through the smoke. Mugwort (*Artemisia vulgaris*), vervain (*Verbena officinalis*), and yarrow (*Achillea millefolium*) are all herbs associated with divination and discernment. [Please note: refrain from using the technology of "smudging" with white sage (*Salvia apiana*) for this purpose unless you have trained with and been given permission by an Indigenous elder.]

Consecrating your tools comes next. Consecration sets the purpose and direction of your relationship with your tools. Simply hold the object in your hand, and speak your intentions for its ethical use. You may want to empower and bless your tools with the five elements—air, fire, water, earth, and spirit. You can breathe on your tools or kiss them to enliven them with your own energy. Make an offering of some kind (such as a song or poem) to symbolize your good intentions for this relationship. Afterward, each time you take the tools out for a scrying session, remember to repeat your chosen action to continue enlivening them.

Many people find it helpful to wrap their scrying tools in silk when not in use. Silk functions as an "energetic insulator" to help protect tools from stray influences. Animal-based fibers (like wool or leather) are recommended if you do not have silk.

Warding Your Space
To begin preparing for a scrying session, select a quiet space that allows for clear focus, and one in which you feel safe. This space can be indoors or outdoors, but it's best to limit distracting sounds and lights. Next, ward the space.

"Warding" is the practice of setting physical and ethereal boundaries to keep harmful influences out of your space while engaging in vulnerable spiritual or energetic work. Warding can also help create a boundary between your personal thoughts and the receptive psychic moment of scrying. The more ceremonial cues you create around your scrying practice, the more effectively you can separate this type of insight from your usual mind chatter.

To ward your space, begin by securing the actual physical area from physical disturbances (close the door, ask roommates not to bother you, draw curtains, etc.). Standing in the center of your space, and pointing outward with your right index finger, slowly turn in a clockwise circle to cast an energetic barrier around you and your scrying tools. The intention of this circle casting is to create a workspace in which you can concentrate freely and safely on your scrying. Once you have turned a full circle, the next step is to place a sign of warding and protection in each of the four cardinal directions (east, south, west, and north) and in the center of the circle. Once again, you can draw this sign with your right index finger, empowering it with the intention of protection. Common warding signs include the pentagram, Norse runes, the equal-armed cross, or a sigil with personal meaning to you.

Allegedly the scrying mirror of 16th Century occultist, John Dee.
Photo courtesy of Science Museum A127914

Once your warding is complete, you may find it helpful to employ some meditative or grounding techniques before beginning a scrying session. Some people find deep breathing exercises focus and quiet the mind. Others find theta wave music (in the 7-6 Hz range) to help induce a trance-like state of concentration. Still yet, others like to open their scrying sessions with prayers or an invocation to an Unseen One (non-corporeal entity) that serves as a patroness or guide for their scrying activities. A few examples of figures from mythology and mystical traditions connected to scrying and divination include Ceridwen (Welsh), Pythia (Greek), Sybil (Greco-Roman), the Norns (Norse), and St. Clare of Assisi (an Italian Catholic saint).

Crafting Your Question

Approaching your scrying session with a specific question can be useful, especially for gaining insight into everyday practicalities. Some examples of specific questions for divination:

"How can I find a used car that will be both reliable and affordable?"

"What should I do about a problem in my relationship?"

"I've been offered a job, how will it impact my life if I accept it?"

When you receive an image, answer, or impression through scrying, trust the message but also verify it. Research the answers and impressions you receive to be sure they actually suggest a good course of action for you.

You can also seek general insight in a scrying session. Without specifics built into your question, sometimes it can seem much harder to interpret the information you receive. However, as a general insight practice, this type of scrying creates space for important tidbits to come through that we would not otherwise have known to ask about. Some examples might include:

"What dynamics should I pay attention to between now and the full moon?"

"What do I need to be aware of that I am overlooking this week?"

THREE MEDIUMS FOR SCRYING: WATER, MIRROR, AND FLAME

Water Scrying

Water scrying begins with a vessel. If you are using a glass, clay, or porcelain bowl, you may want to choose one that has minimal patterns or visual distractions. You can also use a small iron cauldron consecrated for this purpose. Have this vessel on hand, as well as water for your medium.

The basic technique for water scrying:

1. Purify yourself and the area. Set your tools in the center of the circle that you will cast for the scrying session. Dim all lighting.

2. Cast a circle and ward your space.

3. Pour water into your scrying vessel, and enliven it.

4. State your question: "I come to the Water to ask…"

5. Soften your focus. Practice looking through the water's surface as if you are looking through a window to the outside. Keep breathing as necessary.

    a. Images may appear in the water or in your mind's eye. Some people, such as myself, even scry with their eyes closed!

    b. It can be common to see mist, swirls, smoke, horizontal or vertical lines, and simple textures at first. There can be movement or static.

    c. You may not get images… you may get a smell, a sound, a feeling in your body. There are many forms of information. Pay attention to it all, and track it over time so that you can learn what scrying is like for you personally.

    d. Allow impressions to arise without judgment.

6. Record your observations.

7. Close the session verbally: "I thank the Water for its wisdom and insight."

8. Release your circle and wards.

9. Dispose of the water respectfully (such as offering it to a plant or tree).

10. Thank and secure your tools until the next time.

Mirror Scrying

Scrying into a mirror feels "airy" energetically—air represents the realm of communication, mental activity, conflict, isolation, constructs, innovation, inspiration, and the suit of Swords in the Tarot. Whether you create or buy a scrying mirror, you will want to keep considerations like size, aesthetics, and mobility in mind. I created a simple black scrying mirror from a beloved picture frame passed down to me from my maternal grandmother. I simply painted one side of the glass in the frame black, placing the painted side face-down in the frame so that the glossy side of the glass was visible to me. I then removed the hanging hardware from the back of the frame so that it would lie flat on a table.

The basic technique for black mirror scrying:

1. Purify yourself and the area. Set your tools in the center of the circle that you will cast for the scrying session. Dim all lighting.

2. Cast a circle and ward your space.

3. Light two candles, one on either side of the mirror (optional and with safety in mind). Uncover, clean if necessary, and enliven your mirror.

4. State your question: "I come to the Mirror to ask…"

5. Soften your focus. Look through the surface of the mirror as if it were a deep pool of liquid. Keep breathing as necessary.

6. Record your observations.

7. Close the session verbally: "I thank the Mirror for its wisdom and insight."

8. Snuff out the candles.

9. Release your circle and wards.

10. Thank and secure your tools until the next time.

Flame Scrying

To scry into the flames, you must have a fire. Depending on your resources and environment, you can use anything from a small tealight candle to a bonfire. Single flames and roaring fires are equally powerful and insightful! Be sure to have water on hand for safety and matches to conjure the flame.

The basic technique for flame scrying:

1. Purify yourself and the area. Set your tools in the center of the circle that you will cast for the scrying session. Dim all lighting (if applicable).

2. Cast a circle and ward your space.

3. Enliven your scrying tools (candles, dish, hearth, etc.) and light the fire.

4. State your question: "I come to the Fire to ask…"

5. Soften your focus. Keep breathing as necessary. Interpret the dance of the flames.

    a. What color is the flame (i.e., red, orange, blue)?

    b. Is the flame steady or licking low or high?

    c. Is the flame tending toward one direction?

    d. What shapes do you see in the flame? In the shadows?

    e. If you are singing a song to the fire (highly recommended), take note of any remarkable activity corresponding to specific lines of the song or activity corresponding to a specific thought.

6. Record your observations.

7. Close the session verbally: "I thank the Fire for its wisdom and insight."

8. Extinguish the flames.

9. Release your circle and wards.

10. Thank and secure your tools until the next time. Once cooled, dispose of any ashes respectfully (such as offering them to the earth).

CLOSING THOUGHTS

It can be tempting to think any insights or experiences you receive during a scrying session are simply your imagination. But I would invite you to suspend your disbelief, just for the moment, and keep recording. See what takes form over time. The basic techniques of scrying are easy and accessible, but like many art forms, becoming a master usually takes practice… a lot of practice. With time and repetition, you'll figure out what works best for you, and begin to reap the rewards of honing your insight and intuition.

Best of luck with your scrying practice!

References:

Carr-Gomm, Stephanie, and Philip Carr-Gomm. *The Druid Plant Oracle*. St. Martin's Press, 2008.

Guiley, Rosemary Ellen. *The Art of Black Mirror Scrying*. Visionary Living, Incorporated, 2016.

Telyndru, Jhenah. *Avalon Within: A Sacred Journey of Myth, Mystery, and Inner Wisdom*. Llewellyn Publications, 2010.

Louisiana Folklore

Nikki Clement

In my 38 years, I have been a perpetual seeker. I was born with a hunger for all knowledge. The first time I picked up a book about folklore, I couldn't have been any older than nine. It drew me in like the proverbial moth to a flame. By the third page, I was hooked. I gobbled up any information I could find.

I spent countless hours in local libraries learning about folklore from all over the world. I would approach my teachers with a barrage of questions about their knowledge (thank goodness they obliged). I was especially entranced with folklore from my own culture.

We have such rich and varied history here in Louisiana. It's almost impossible to visit any town without coming upon a legend. I believe those legends are worth saving... Protecting.

Settle in, and let's have a good time while I tell you a good tale.

THE ROUGAROU

One of the most well-known legends of south Louisiana is the Rougarou. The Rougarou is what some would consider Louisiana's version of a werewolf. The original story has changed over time in many ways. In some versions, it's a human put under a curse for 101 days by a Voodoo priestess or local witch. The affected person is said to be able to transfer the curse to someone else if blood is drawn. This was said to be accomplished by cutting their arm or hand. You can protect yourself against the Rougarou by laying 13 small objects by your doors or windows. The Rougarou will see the 13 objects, try to count them, and be unable to count them all. This will confuse it, and it will keep recounting until the sun comes up, and it must flee back into the bayou.

In other versions, it is simply a beast who hunts down and kills anyone not following the rules of Lent.

In yet a third version, it is a spirit that can inhabit almost anything—a tried-and-true shapeshifter. Native legends have included it among their guardians.

It was in this form I had a personal encounter with as a child. Whatever it may be, whatever form it may take, it would be wise to be truthful and go to bed when told, or the Rougarou just may get you.

The Grunch Road Monster

The earliest reports of this creature date back to the Louisiana Purchase in 1803.

This creature seems to prefer staying around the New Orleans area. Legend has it that the Grunch dates back to the days of New Orleans' early settlement and that its name "Grunch" comes from the name of a road. This Southern cryptid has been called The Vampire of Farbourgh Marigny and Bywater Area, dating back to the early 1800s. The Legend of Marie Laveau tells of how some believe this form of Chupacabra came into existence.

Old Voodoo stories say Marie Laveau castrated the Devil Baby when he was born to keep him from producing more of his kind. The bloody testicles allegedly turned into a male and a female Grunch upon falling to the floor before they attacked the great Voodoo Queen. The Grunch are said to have almost killed her with their ferocity. Legend claims that she fainted, and the Grunch and the Devil Baby were gone when she awoke.

The most common description of the Grunch is a goat-like being, appearing to have leathery or scaly black-gray skin and sharp spines with long horns or quills running down its back. This creature stands

approximately three to four feet tall. They are also said to seem more intelligent and have human-like skills. It is said to howl like a wolf, leaving behind a strong stench. Reports have mentioned glowing red or blue-green eyes. Evidence of it draining the blood of its victims is an earmark of its presence.

Some people claim it was in Chalmette, Louisiana, while others claim it was in Gentilly or Metairie—but the "real" Grunch Road is located in a remote part of Eastern New Orleans near the community of Little Woods.

Stories of floating lights and strange screams in the night continue to this very day. Photos of a creature alleged to be the Grunch have surfaced over recent years, keeping the legend of Grunch Road alive to this day.

THE LEGEND OF *LE FEU FOLLET*

Feu Follet translates to "marsh light," "swamp fire," or "will-o-the-wisp."

Many Cajuns would tell you today that their grandparents or ancestors would share stories of the mysterious orbs of light glowing— almost beckoning you to go and find them on the darkest of nights in the bayou. Those who witnessed this phenomenon dubbed them "swamp fairies," aka *le feu follet*. They are described as bright or flickering balls of light randomly dancing in the dark shadows of the bayou. They've supposedly been seen in different sizes, but the average size is said to be no larger than a candle flame.

The *feu follet* was sometimes identified as the spirits of dead loved ones coming back to say their final goodbyes. This had a semblance of peace, assuring the Cajuns that their loved ones were visiting them and bringing good fortune.

In other cases, these glowing balls of light were said to be evil spirits laying a trap for those unfortunate enough to stumble upon them. The balls of light were thought to be a lure in hopes that someone would be drawn to them and go deep into the swamp to get lost or drown. Due to their sinister nature, families would tell their children never to follow the lights, no matter what.

According to some lore, the *feu follet* cannot cross iron. This is one of the reasons they are so closely associated with fairies. Plenty of accounts paint these entities as small people holding lanterns gesturing for the unsuspecting traveler to follow them.

Modern times have uncovered that the origin of these lights may simply be swamp gas (specifically methane) burning off in the environment, but there are still accounts in places you may not expect.

One of the most well-known tales comes from a Lake Charles, Louisiana cemetery, where glowing orbs of light float with intelligence around the headstones. These reports started in the 1840s and continue to this very day.

It definitely puts "leaving a light on" for visitors into a new perspective, doesn't it?

THE LEGEND OF ONION HEAD

The legend of Onion Head begins about 60 years ago in Slidell, Louisiana. There was said to be a giant of a man who roamed the woods, lived with his mother, and was seldom seen in public. A childhood disease disfigured him, and the locals had given him the cruel nickname of Onion Head.

One day, a young girl was found murdered in the woods. The locals decided amongst themselves that Onion Head must have killed her. Before the police had a chance to launch an investigation, they formed a mob and went to the home of Onion Head. When he saw the crowd coming for him, he fled into the woods. His mother tried to reason with the townspeople, but it was no use as they thirsted for justice. She threatened to put a curse on anyone who harmed her son.

The mob hunted Onion Head down and found him hiding in a ditch. Filled with rage, they killed him and dismembered his corpse. Legend has it they cut him into 13 pieces and buried him throughout the local graveyard.

Soon after, the police captured the young girl's actual murderer—a drifter who had been passing through town at the time. The townsfolk quickly realized Onion Head was innocent.

As time passed, there were a series of grisly murders in town. The victims all had the same thing in common: every one of them had been part of the mob that killed Onion Head. At every crime scene, a message was written in blood. It read, "If you were there, I'm coming to kill you too." The message was signed as none other than Onion Head.

According to the legends, Onion Head is the perpetual caretaker of the Haaswood Cemetery in Slidell. He enacted his revenge on those who wronged him and now lies in wait for anyone else foolish enough to linger too long in the cemetery.

MADAME GRAND DOIGT

Madame Grand Doigt translates to "lady with the long fingers." Like many of the legends in South Louisiana, it is based on making children behave and listen to their parents. Also common with many folktales: every family or generation has its own version to tell. Madame is no exception. Depending on your family or where you grew up, she might make you laugh or cry.

For many children, they were told she was an evil witch who lived in the attic. The actual origin and identity of this long-fingered lady are much different. According to legend, she was originally known as *la fille aux belles mains* ("the young lady with beautiful hands"). She was the belle of the town, and all men wanted to court her. This led to jealousy from the other young women, so they lured her to a party and put  a gris-gris on her beautiful hands. The following day when she awoke, she discovered her once lovely, flawless hands were now gnarled and covered in warts. Ashamed and heartbroken, she fled to her attic and never again returned to the public eye. Ever since, her ghost has gone from attic to attic, haunting anyone who comes within reach.

Some interpretations have Madame prowling around roads and trails in the bayou, kidnapping mischievous children. She throws them into her sack, collecting their toes for a necklace and other nefarious purposes. Creepily, no one knows what happens to the children from there.

Other legends have *Madame Grand Doigts* as a sweet gift-giving woman. According to some, she brings gifts to children on Christmas Eve. In this version of the tale, she uses her long spindly fingers to place little gifts in the stockings of good girls and boys.

Whether friend or foe, I think it's better to stay on *Madame Grand Doigts'* good side!

These are just a few of our legends here in Louisiana, and I'm happy you have stayed with me this long. The fire is getting low, and sleep must come for us all. Remember the lessons these stories have taught you on your journeys home or as you pass into your dreams:

Not everything is always as it seems.

Don't follow any beckoning lights or strangers.

Stay on the lighted pathways.

Attics aren't the best place to go and hide during games.

Say a prayer of protection, and go forth into the good night.

References:

https://pelicanstateofmind.com/louisiana-love/history-rougarou-louisiana-werewolf/

https://cryptidz.fandom.com/wiki/Grunch_Road_Monster

https://aminoapps.com/c/cryptid-and-mysteries-amino/page/item/grunch-road-monster/PJLq_EKjH3I6aRrG0n5E0pGGVeM1VPwx7qW

https://pelicanstateofmind.com/louisiana-love/mystery-louisiana-feu-follet/

https://deepdarkforestblog.wordpress.com/2016/11/23/film/

https://www.scaryforkids.com/onion-head/

https://wgno.com/news/entertainment/hometown-horror-stories-onionhead/

https://countryroadsmagazine.com/art-and-culture/people-places/madame-grands-doigts/

Hung from a Common Scaffold

Maria Blair

If you visit Niagara Square in Buffalo today, you'll stand in the shadow of an Art Deco masterpiece of a city hall, a literal monument to a turn of the last century American president (cut down mere blocks away by an assassin's bullet), an incredibly modern federal court building, and countless other historic, architectural ornaments giving us glimpses of times gone by. However, nearly 200 years before the court building was constructed, almost 100 years before a new city hall was even a thought, and before a single piece of this square existed, all that stood here was little more than the public gallows.

This location, which today is often bustling with 9-5 traffic during the week and with casual tourists and locals alike on weekends, was once the location of Buffalo's only public hanging. The story leading up to this event is sordid, unfortunate, and at times downright ridiculous. It begins 20 miles south in the quiet town of Boston, New York.

Buffalo, NY's Art Deco masterpiece city hall, 2004.
Photo courtesy of T.C. Weichmann

The brothers Thayer: Israel, Isaac, and Nelson were all born around 1800 in Massachusetts. Their father, Israel Sr., moved the family to Boston, New York, when his sons were around 10 to 15 years old. Though this may be in hindsight of the events to come, it was said that their father regretted not having raised his sons in a moral way, neglecting their education. Neighbors would say they used the Lord's name in vain, stole fruit, and gambled.

The brothers would grow into young men and soon have their own farms and families. Still, they seemed more interested in participating in the more scandalous, rough and tumble aspects of life than in living as fine upstanding gentleman farmers. They were more interested in drinking and shooting matches than in a hard day's work. And so it was of little surprise that all three were in tremendous debt by their early 20s.

Enter John Love, an Irish sailor who wintered in Boston and worked on ships navigating the Great Lakes for the remainder of the year. As a young, single seafarer who only needed to provide for his own living arrangements a fraction of the year, he seemed to be financially comfortable. In fact, John held enough disposable income that he often made loans to other townsfolk in the area. And some of his largest debtors were the Thayer brothers.

John seemed quite the liberal creditor in that he allowed the brothers to use future crops as collateral and loaned them at least $275 (over $8,000 today) as this was the amount still owed to him in 1824 when there was a judgment brought against the Thayers.

Isaac, Israel, and Nelson were in tremendous debt to various lenders. However, this debt from Mr. Love hung over their heads and caused them sleepless nights. This debt was their most significant and the most likely to prove their collective demise. The brothers seemed to be in considerable danger of losing their property and only means of making a living to John.

So, in the weeks leading up to that winter, the three began planning the unspeakable. They knew of only one way to get out from under their suffocating debt. The only possible ending to all this was to take John's life, and on December 15th, the brothers set out to do just that.

An elaborate plan was soon in place, where each brother would play his part. The death would be quick and the disposal of the body simple. Or so they believed.

As nightfall approached, Israel came to Nelson and Isaac (who were in the company of John Love at the time) to ask for their assistance in cutting and preserving the meat from some of his hogs that he had butchered earlier that day. John, Isaac, and Nelson were at Nelson's home, per the later testimony of Nelson's wife. They would then travel to Israel's home to make a night of getting the meat preserved and ready for the coming winter months.

Apparently, John not only felt comfortable enough to spend the evening and late-night hours in the company of men severely overdrawn in their debts to him, but he was at ease enough to remove his hat, coat, shoes, and even his stockings, before relaxing in a chair inside the home.

Earlier that day, Israel had loaded a rifle and placed it near a tree in the yard, in direct view of a window John now sat with his back to. While Nelson and Israel conversed with John, Isaac made some pretext to go outside and then made his way to the rifle. He aimed the gun and shot clear through the window and into the back of John's head. To all three brothers' surprise, John did not immediately die. In a panic, Nelson grabbed a nearby ax and struck John several times until he succumbed to the wounds.

Israel and Nelson brought the body out of the home. All three cleaned the house as best they could, even bringing in some of the hogs' meat to lay on John's chair (the hogs actually were butchered earlier that day). They thought this could explain away the blood stains should anyone ask.

Isaac then left for home, and the other two buried the body. They decided to bury him on the property, near a brook and a footpath. It was mid-December in New York State, and by this point, the rugged rocky soil was made even less manageable by the cold beginning to harden the ground. So, the pair only ended up burying the body 14 to 16 inches deep and covering it with even less dirt.

In the coming days, the brothers would take full advantage of not only John's absence but also of his worldly goods, giving little credence to propriety. All three paid off their other creditors with John's stolen funds, and still, there was more to spare. Witnesses would later speak of the brothers flashing large amounts of cash and buying expensive items after John's disappearance.

The Thayers even went so far as to tell the other townsfolk that John Love had absconded to Canada because he was escaping the law for an offense he'd committed in Pennsylvania. The brothers soon decided that they could profit even further from John's demise. Together, they forged a power of attorney showing that John had settled their debt and given them rights to collect on debts others had owed to John Love. The document also stated that they had purchased these debts from John before he had fled the country.

However, as can be imagined, this all seemed entirely too coincidental and convenient to those in town, and suspicious talk soon made its way from home to home. Many noted last seeing John in the company of Nelson at his home on that fateful night of the 15th of December. Others mentioned seeing the pair heading for Israel's home that evening, John easily recognizable in his famous greatcoat. Still more recalled hearing gunshots that night. Another damning fact was that Israel Thayer had lately been seen in possession of John Love's horse, and his paperwork was with Isaac. It seemed strange that a man headed North to escape authorities wouldn't see fit to travel with his horse, especially in leaving a small town such as Boston. Perhaps, the most chilling thing that put the brothers under suspicion was a comment Isaac made to someone questioning the power of attorney that they were using. Trying to explain John's whereabouts, he stated, "My God, Love is farther from this country than anybody has any idea of."

By February, locals began searching for a body, fearing the worst. And it wasn't long at all before one was found. Not only was John buried near a footpath and on Israel's property, but because of that frozen, rocky soil, he was buried so shallowly (the story goes) that his toes were sticking out of the ground. Other accounts reference the reason for the body's discovery was only that the ground looked to be recently disturbed.

"The body appeared to be crowded into the grave," per an article written by the *Buffalo Emporium and General Advertiser* that spring during the trial. Once the body began to be uncovered, John's greatcoat was one of the first things to appear under the rocky earth. The body was severely damaged, but after a coroner's inquest at a nearby schoolhouse, it was quickly determined to be the missing Irish sailor. The inquest, which occurred on February 24th, stated that there was a bullet hole just below the left eye that would have caused death, though not instantaneously, since it did not pass directly through the brain. Other wounds on or about the head (of which there were many) seemed to have been caused by an ax or other similar object. The skull had been fractured into a dozen pieces, and the neck was broken.

Two of the brothers, Nelson and Isaac, who were more heavily involved in the forged power of attorney scheme and who had wielded the gun and ax (though the authorities did not know this at the time), were arrested on suspicion of John's murder on the 20th, three days before the body was discovered. It was thought that more family members were involved. Ultimately, all three brothers and their father were arrested and brought to Buffalo for trial since that was the location for murder trials in Erie County (of which Boston was a part).

They were sent to Buffalo's courthouse, which once stood in the current location of the downtown branch of the Buffalo and Erie County Public Library. All three brothers were brought up on charges of murder. Their father would be acquitted quickly of the same charge, but indictments for concealing the crime were considered for some time. However, it is difficult to determine whether he was ever tried for anything related to Love's murder.

The brothers found a competent defense attorney in a man who coincidently carried the same surname as their victim (but was of no relation)—Thomas C. Love. He would argue that the evidence against his clients was entirely circumstantial. Three witnesses last saw John in the brothers' company (often citing the greatcoat), including Nelson's wife. She made it very clear that though she heard Israel ask her husband about cutting the hog's meat and he did ask John to join them, she heard no talk of a rifle. She also stated that her husband was out all night, but this was common. Several testified to the gunshots heard and to the inauthenticity of the power of attorney, citing that Love's signature did not look like his own. Still, Thomas Love argued that none of this directly proved that the brothers were actually guilty of murder.

Unfortunately, for Isaac, Israel, and Nelson, the jury in Buffalo did not find credibility in this argument. The facts stacked up against the Thayers and only one explanation for John's death seemed likely. The jury deliberated for 30 minutes in the trial of Israel and Isaac before returning with a verdict of guilty on April 25th. Nelson was tried on the next day, separate from his two brothers so that his wife's testimony could be used in the trial of his brothers since it could not be used against him, but the result was the same in both cases.

During sentencing, the judge remarked on how dark a day it was when he was forced to condemn men that (as he put it) were at the beginnings of life to death. He gave a lengthy speech describing the effects of the horrific crime on the brothers' parents, wives, and children. He ended by stating: "And may that God whose laws you have broken and before whose dread tribunal you must then appear, have mercy on your souls!"

They would be sentenced to death by hanging from a common scaffold. The execution date was set for the middle of June.

In the nearly eight weeks spanning the time between sentencing and death, the brothers would give a full confession of the events of the crime. It seems this detailed account was given partly to help prove that Israel Sr. had no knowledge of the crimes. It was said that Nelson and Isaac were resigned to their fate, but Israel, not having participated in the actual killing, did not see himself as truly guilty of murder. All three did use those weeks to read scripture and seek penance.

On the morning of June 17, 1825, just six months after their crime, the Thayer brothers prepared for what would be a dramatic public death. In the days leading to it, people had begun to make their way to the area. It was said that "all the roads leading to Buffalo were thronged with men, women, and children pressing to the scene of the death."

And at a time when Buffalo's population was around 2,000, it was believed that between 20,000-30,000 clamored together as close as possible to where the gallows stood (in what is now Niagara Square).

At noon the brothers were led out of the courthouse, dressed in their white burial shrouds. The ominous music of a death march went through the streets with them as they made their way by foot from the courthouse straight through the gathered masses of on-lookers. They would travel ahead of the heavy plod of a wagon carrying their own coffins.

Once the brothers arrived and made their way up the scaffold, a sermon and prayer were given by a local reverend, and their full confession was read. Isaac, Israel, and Nelson stood together patiently listening, perhaps looking into the crowd for their families, including a mother whom they would not find. She had died after they were convicted, some would say of a broken heart. It had been decided not to tell the brothers as her death was so shortly before the certainty of their own. All were loath to add more pain in their final days.

When the time came, two hours had passed since the brothers had first begun their journey from the courthouse to the gallows. At precisely two in the afternoon, a prayer was said as the nooses were tied. It was noted that the floor went out from under the brothers' feet as Nelson was still in mid-prayer. All three died together in that square as the only public hanging in the city of Buffalo or the county of Erie. All four men, including John, had been in their 20s, all had presumably long lives ahead of them, and all four died over a payable debt.

References:

Buffalo Emporium and General Advertiser, Saturday, May 7, 1825, pg. 3

Buffalo Emporium and General Advertiser, Saturday, May 14, 1825, pg. 2

Buffalo Emporium and General Advertiser, Saturday, June 25, 1825, pg. 3

"Execution of the Thayers," Black Rock Gazette, Tuesday, June 21, 1825, pg. 3

Robert Wilhelm, "The Thayer Brothers," Murder By Gaslight May 21, 2011, http://www.murderbygaslight.com/2011/05/thayer-brothers.html

"The trial of the Thayers," Buffalo Emporium and General Advertiser, Saturday, April 30, 1825, pg. 2-3

"Trials for Murder," Black Rock Gazette, Tuesday, April 26, 1825, pg. 3

Are You a Good Witch or a Bad Witch?

Ann Marie West

Good vs. Evil: it's been a fight since the beginning of time. Sometimes it's played out on a battlefield between large armies, but most often, it's played out within each of us individually.

Recently I was at a psychic fair and walked by a table with beautiful boxed kits. Drawn in by the presentation, I stopped and took a closer look. On the left half of the table, the boxes had items with darker colors—obsidian points, black candles, and a sign asking, "Are You a Bad Witch?" The right side had white candles, selenite, and (you guessed it) a sign which read, "Are You a Good Witch?"

Immediately, I felt my blood boil like a cauldron over an open flame. First, obsidian is used for grounding, healing, and protection. I personally have a large chunk of it under my bed. Black does not automatically equal bad. In candle magic, black candles are used for banishing, releasing, endings, clearing negativity, and cleansing. So what exactly was this vendor trying to sell? Maybe trying to neutralize a so-called "Bad Witch?" A true practitioner of the dark arts would walk right on by with a chuckle and raised brow. There was also an option to get a monthly subscription depending on which kind of witch you identified as. So, once you decide, that's it.

After calming down, I had to ask myself why I was so angry. Because she was misusing tools? Taking advantage of people new to the craft? Was it because she was asking people to identify themselves as good or bad? The answer is all of the above. The Wiccan community has been judged since its inception—why do we judge ourselves and others so harshly? Plus, we live in a capitalist society with the motto of "buyer-beware" firmly planted in our heads from the time we start spending our hard-earned money.

Witches have been living on the edges of their community for centuries or hiding in plain sight in fear of being discovered. In the past, they did not self-identify as witches but as healers, shamans, wise-people, hermits, etc. They were midwives, helping new babies enter the world. Healers assisting people with ailments. Some had the "sight" and told fortunes. Different cultures had different names and roles for them. The one thing they all had in common was they often lived on the fringe of society—a society that did not want them living among them yet would often visit them when they needed their help. If a baby died or someone could not be healed, grief could turn to condemnation and an accusation of witchcraft. Societal ills were blamed on those living on the fringe. Most importantly, they were people—our ancestors—that laid the foundation for where we are today.

Hollywood has created a whole cadre of witchy stereotypes. My first experience with a "witch" was *The Wizard of Oz* (flying monkeys still terrify me to this day... although I must admit, I have never seen them anywhere other than on a television screen). *The Exorcist, The Omen,* and *The Craft* scared me. *Practical Magic* was lovely. However, *Bewitched* was my absolute favorite. I always wanted to be Serena, Samantha's naughty cousin, have a daughter, and name her Tabitha.

In *The Wizard of Oz*, Glinda, the Good Witch of the North, asks Dorothy if she is a good witch or a bad witch. Dorothy replies, "Who me? I'm not a witch at all." Glinda is dressed in a beautiful pale-pink gown, is loved by all in the land, and ascends upwards towards the heavens in a bubble. While the Wicked Witch of the West rides a broomstick through dark skies, has a black dress and pointed hat, green skin, a curved warty nose, and flying monkeys under her control. The difference is made clear by their outfits, lighting, and the music played for each. "Good" and "bad" were visually and audibly so clearly different that my five-year-old self knew whom to love and fear.

Anyway, the "Bad Witch" boxes were selling out (or perhaps the vendor had made less of them). They were attracting more attention than the "Good Witch" boxes as I watched people stop by the table and purchase them.

It is hard to define yourself. Labels are hard. There are so many choices. It is difficult for most to come out of the broom closet, much less decide to go down a path that is either "Good" or "Bad."

> PATHS USUALLY WIND ONE WAY AND THEN ANOTHER. GOOD AND BAD ARE SUBJECTIVE WITH ONE HOPEFULLY BALANCING THE OTHER.

There are also many terms: witch, warlock, wizard, psychic, medium, Wiccan, pagan… the list goes on. These terms are often used incorrectly (spoiler alert: a male witch is not a warlock). Historically, males were charged with being a witch, not with being a warlock.

In a field plagued by fraud and tricksters since its inception, why let this trickster in the midst? It is the equivalent of allowing a vendor to set up shop and sell pieces of the crucifix or the Shroud of Turin outside the Vatican. It is sacrilegious. However, was she truly being deceitful? After all, magick is about intent. If the buyer believes they are a "Bad Witch," then aren't they? What happens if a black candle is used with "bad" intent? Will it be "bad?" Theoretically, yes. They will be changing the accepted norms of these tools of the craft and making them their own.

> ISN'T THAT WHAT PRACTITIONERS HAVE BEEN DOING FOR THOUSANDS OF YEARS? LIVING OUTSIDE THE ACCEPTED NORMS OF SOCIETY? USING WHAT THEY HAVE ON HAND AND USING INTENTION TO CAST THEIR SPELL?

After all, just like Glinda told Dorothy in *The Wizard of Oz*, "You had the power all along, my dear." She just had to click her heels three times and say, "There's no place like home." Dorothy simply had to use the tools given to her (the shoes) and state her intention.

Perhaps I am merely following those that have come before me, like a docile sheep. Who decided what the black candle and the obsidian stood for and what their correspondences were anyway? After all, in some cultures, red is a funerary color, not black. So, does it really matter? Perhaps the people purchasing the "Bad Witch" box are being the black sheep, the true magickal practitioner, going off in their own direction, forging a new magickal path. Perhaps they are more like our ancestors than I.

Who am I to be a spiritual gatekeeper for a community? Who am I to judge?

Besides, I did always want to be Serena, the naughty witch. Maybe I should go see if there are any "Bad Witch" boxes left… at the very least, I could always use another piece of obsidian!

Representation Matters: Non-Binary Authors

[Editor's Note: Since our second volume, we have opened submissions to those who identify as non-binary. The purpose of *The Feminine Macabre* is to provide a space for underrepresented groups to share their research, thoughts, and theories. We're honored to have these talented researchers join us in this journal.]

Regaining the Power in Feminine Shapeshifting

Nashoba Hostina

"If the men find out that we can shape-shift, they're going to tell the church!"

This quote is from the YouTube channel, D.C.'s Video Archive, and the video in question is Contouring 101. This particular audio clip seems to have taken off on the short-form video platform TikTok, and is often used by feminine creators putting on makeup to appear as otherworldly creatures. The appearance may only be skin deep, but these transformations are painstaking, artful, and a means of self-expression worthy of awe.

Yet, in modern western culture, when someone thinks of a shapeshifter, they are most likely to consider the werewolf, a role often attributed to men. The transition from man to beast is sometimes portrayed as a bid for pity, a tragedy as man falls victim to the strength of his own violent and primal urges, or, in better scenarios, a power fantasy in which the wild inside is worn as a wolf skin

and utilized to his own exhilarating gain.

That said, while it is somewhat unusual to see women as the leads in werewolf stories, there certainly are a few good folklore examples, such as the infamous Perrnette Gandillion, a witch who attacked children while in the guise of a wolf, or Claudia Gaillard, who became a wolf while collecting alms with a companion. In modern times, there are a few good examples, such as the *Kitty and the Midnight Hour* book series, featuring a plucky female werewolf as the protagonist, or the film *Cursed*… Yet even there, the fact that the werewolf was a woman was treated as a twist, the film deliberately set the audience up to think that the stereotypical male suspect was the werewolf until the end.

> IN FACT, IN MUCH OF MEDIA AND FOLKLORE, WHEN WOMEN ARE SHAPESHIFTERS, IT IS OFTENTIMES ABOUT A LOSS OF POWER, RATHER THAN AN EXAMPLE OF IT.

This may be because our society, dominated by the masculine gaze, often finds powerful, bestial women unpalatable. After all, while I would argue that the tale of Medusa in Ovid's *Metamorphoses* would be more of a transformational tale rather than a shape-shifting story, even there, when the woman in question experienced severe trauma, ending in her gaining a shape that happened to bring her protection from the gaze of men, she was eventually slain for it.

A kinder story may be that of Melusine, a beautiful woman of fairy lineage who had been cursed by her mother to, at times, be a serpent from the waist down. She agreed to marry on the sole condition that her husband did

Melusine *by Heinrich Vogeler, c.1912*

not look upon her at certain times—most notably Saturdays (though the tale varies). I have also heard variants where the boundary she required was absolute privacy while bathing, instead. Unfortunately, her husband betrays her trust and sees her bestial form, which ultimately leads to heartbreak.

However, it is sometimes found that shapeshifter stories in folklore will have a man remove a shapeshifter's power so that he may wed them. In fact, in Thompson's folkloric motif index, the marriage to an animal in human form has its own category. While this category does include marriage to animals in human form for both men and women, in my personal experience, one of the more impactful stories was that of the swan maiden.

Like all such stories, the tale varies, though a short version is that a man comes across a swan maiden who, having taken off her feather garments, in this vulnerable state, appears as a beautiful woman. The man of the story then steals her swan cloak and hides it away, robbing her both of her freedom as well as her agency of appearance. This leaves her in his power until she is able to reclaim her skin and fly away, leaving her suitor behind.

The Swan Maidens *by Walter Crane, 1894.*

Even in the few werewolf tales involving women, they can have their power of *versipellis* (the means to change one's skin at their own will) taken from them. For instance, Gerald of Wales's *Topographia Hibernica* weaves a tale in Ossory, where a male werewolf in lupine form convinces a priest to give last rites to a she-wolf, but only after her wolfskin has been pulled aside by him. Once the priest can see the helpless, dying woman underneath, only then does he assist. It may be worth noting that the priest did not request the male werewolf to prove his humanity.

The donning and removal of animal pelts to change one's shape and appearance can be analogous to the fashion choices women may make today.

> THE WOLFSKIN IS A SOURCE OF POWER WORN BY THE SHAPESHIFTER, LIKE MAKEUP, A DRESS WITH THIN SHOULDER STRAPS, A SPIKED LEATHER VEST, OR A BUSINESS SUIT.

So often, women's clothing is policed by those around them to encourage the comfort and enjoyment of men. Yet, so often, when a woman feels empowered enough to wear the metaphorical wolfskin of her choice, men's voices try to evaluate the virtue (or lack thereof) in these choices.

The demeaning and hurtful remarks that women often hear about how they choose to appear could be compared to the thoughts of the German occultist Agrippa, who discussed instances in which what he deems to be superior or inferior virtues may affect one another. According to his writings, the skin of the wolf will corrode the skin of a lamb, and after all, from his perspective, why wouldn't it? There were several instances of lycanthropic rituals in Europe involving even a little of such fur, belts, or girdles made from wolfskin to assist in the transformation.

With all of this in mind, one may wonder what is to be done about it all, and the answer is predictably complicated.

A good course of action for those who excel in creative tasks would be to begin depicting some female shapeshifters in a light intended for women rather than men. Produce creations that are unconventionally attractive but strong and protective, shapeshifters that evoke a sense of freedom and safety rather than desirability.

For those who are metaphysically inclined, engage in shape-shifting practices that may or may not honor feminine qualities. Find the unconventional qualities in animals often considered masculine and the powerful qualities found in animals often considered feminine. Unapologetically invoke the might of whatever animals may be empowering to embody, even if only in non-corporeal ways.

Then, for consumers of media, share and support content with women shapeshifters who break previously established feminine roles and appearances.

Of course, if none of these appeal to you, you could always simply choose to wear the wolfskin you desire, metaphorically or otherwise.

References:

Summers, Montague. *The Werewolf in Lore and Legend* (Dover Books on the Occult). Illustrated, Dover Publications, 2003. 122.

Agrippa, Cornelius. *Agrippa's Occult Philosophy: Natural Magic* (Dover Books on the Occult). Illustrated, Dover Publications, 2006. 87.

Dubois, Pierre, et al. *The Great Encyclopedia of Faeries*. Simon & Schuster, 2006. 117.

Baring-Gould, Sabine. *The Book of Werewolves*. London, Smith, Elder and Co, 1865. 59, 111.

Matthews, John, and Caitlin Matthews. *The Element Encyclopedia of Magical Creatures: The Ultimate A-Z of Fantastic Beings from Myth and Magic*. HarperElement, 2005. 389-90.

PARANORMAL HERSTORY

PAMELA COLMAN SMITH:
A MOST ABNORMALLY PSYCHIC
ARTIST

With over 100 million copies of her iconic tarot deck circulating through more than 20 countries, one would expect the name of Pamela Colman Smith to be familiar with every occultist, paranormal researcher, and practitioner of tarot reading. Sadly, that is not the case. Also known as "Pixie," Pamela Colman Smith illustrated over 20 books (including Bram Stoker's final novel, *The Lair of the White Worm*), wrote two books on Jamaican folklore, edited two magazines, ran Green Sheaf Press which focused on the underrepresented work of female writers of the time, and designed a tarot deck for fellow occultist, Arthur Edward Waite. Today, the world's most successful tarot deck is commonly known as the Rider-Waite tarot deck, seemingly erasing one-half of the creative team from the narrative.

Pamela Colman Smith was born in Central London on February 16, 1878. She was the only child of American merchants Charles Edward Smith and Corinne Colman. When she was 10 years old, the family moved to Kingston, Jamaica, where Pamela was introduced to Obeah and folktales such as Anansi the Spider.

By 1893, she had moved to Brooklyn, New York, and at just 15 years old, she attended the Pratt Institute. It was there that she studied art under Arthur Wesley Dow. At this time, she was heavily influenced by the Arts and Crafts Movement, Symbolism, and Romanticism and even designed her famous signature that would later be found on almost all of her tarot illustrations.

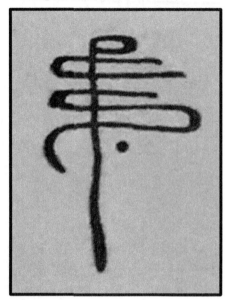

While away at art school, Pamela's mother died in Jamaica in 1896. The following year, after a series of illnesses, Pamela left Pratt without a degree. Just two years later, in 1899, her father would also die, leaving Pamela without either parent at just 21 years old.

Around this time, Pamela began her professional career as an illustrator. Some of her earliest projects included *The Illustrated Verses of William Butler Yeats*, a book about famous actress Ellen Terry written by Bram Stoker, as well as two of her own books. Shortly after her father's death, Pamela returned to England and joined the Lyceum Theatre Company. There, she began traveling the country with Ellen Terry (said to have given Pamela the nickname "Pixie"), Bram Stoker, and actor Henry Irving, designing sets and costumes.

Pamela Colman Smith seated in a theatrical setting, 1903. Artist unknown.

In 1901, Pamela established a studio in London and held weekly open houses for artists, authors, and actors. In 1903, she launched her magazine, which ran for 13 issues over the course of a year. From 1904 to 1906, she ran her small press that published women's novels, poems, folktales, and even fairy tales. By 1907, her paintings were displayed at Alfred Stieglitz's Little Gallery of the Photo-Secession—a gallery originally exclusive to photography.

While running her studio in London, W.B. Yeats introduced Pamela to the Hermetic Order of the Golden Dawn. Also sometimes known as simply "the Golden Dawn," Pamela officially joined the Isis-Urania Temple in 1901.

The Golden Dawn was devoted to the practice of the occult, metaphysics, and paranormal research and incorporated the studies of scrying, alchemy, astrology, and tarot divination. Drawing ideas from Kabbalah and freemasonry, the Golden Dawn was unlike other secret societies of the time because it admitted women and saw them as equal to men. The Golden Dawn saw its height at the end of the

Sea Creatures *watercolor on paper, c.1907.*

19th Century and through the early years of the 20th Century with other notable members such as actress and suffragist, Florence Farr, ghost story author and radio broadcaster, Algernon Blackwood, magician, Aleister Crowley, and British writer and Freemason, Arthur Edward Waite.

During their shared time in the Isis-Urania Temple, A.E. Waite and Pamela Colman Smith met.

Waite described Pamela as "a most imaginative and abnormally psychic artist." And he wasn't too far off.

It is believed that Pamela had a neurological condition called synesthesia that aided her in her artwork. The images she created resulted from what she saw when listening to music:

> "What I wish to make plain is that these are not
> pictures of the music themes […] but just what I see
> when I hear music. Thoughts loosened and set free
> by the spell of sound […] Subconscious energy lives
> in them all."

It was in 1909 that Waite commissioned Pamela to produce a tarot deck for him. It would take Pamela six months (April to October) to illustrate the 78-card deck. According to Pamela, it was a "big job for very little cash," and as it would also turn out very little credit.

Pamela's illustrated cards were simply called *Tarot Cards* when they were published in London by William Rider & Son in December 1909, and Waite's guide was called *The Key to the Tarot*. And while Waite went on to experience fame and fortune, Pamela has been seemingly forgotten despite the majority of the deck's design coming from her talent and creativity.

Many historians believe that Waite was heavily involved with the Major Arcana cards' designs (including The Fool, The Lovers, Death, The Moon, etc.). Waite most likely offered a simple list of meanings for the Minor Arcana cards (also known as "pip" cards). It was Pamela that designed a scene for each of the pip cards, something that had never been done before. Of the 78 cards, 56 came exclusively from Pamela. Some of the figures featured in the deck are even portraits of some of Pamela's friends, including Ellen Terry as the Queen of Wands and Florence Farr as The World.

Actress Ellen Terry as the Queen of Wands.

Florence Farr as The World.

In *Pictures in Music*, Pamela explained:

"When I take a brush in hand, and the music begins, it is like unlocking a door to a beautiful country […] with plains, mountains, and the billowing sea."

Despite the amount of time and energy Pamela put into her illustrations for Waite, her contribution was seemingly wiped out when the deck was sold to US Games in 1971. It was released as the Rider Tarot Deck (named after the [male] publisher), and today, it is wrongfully known as the Rider-Waite deck, excluding half of its creators. Luckily, 21st Century historians exclusively refer to it as the Waite-Smith tarot to recognize Pamela's hard work and contribution while trying to restore her place in the tarot's history.

Over 100 years later, the Waite-Smith deck is still the most popular deck used by tarot readers.

In 1911, Pamela left behind the world of the occult and converted to Catholicism. While this may seem like a jarring leap to some, it's believed by many historians that Pamela joined the Catholic Church for her love of ritual and not the dogma. After all, she had been raised as a Swedenborgian (based on the writings of scientist and mystic Emanuel Swedenborg), was introduced to Obeah while in  Jamaica (a system of spiritual healing similar to Haitian Voodoo), claimed to see fairies the first time she visited Ireland, and joined the Golden Dawn in her 20s. Her belief system was like a patchwork quilt based on her travels and experiences.

Shortly after her conversion, Pamela fell on hard times. With the onset of World War I followed by the Great Depression, work as an artist was hard to come by. She continued to create artwork for the war effort and help with Britain's suffragist movement, but she would never again find the success she experienced during the early 20th Century.

After World War I, she bought a cottage in Cornwall with the help of an inheritance she received from an uncle. Throughout the 1930s and 1940s, she moved around England and continued to experience financial problems.

Pamela Colman Smith died penniless in her apartment on September 18, 1951, at 73 years old. Her artwork and possessions were auctioned off in an attempt to repay her debts. Today, the location of her grave is unknown—she was likely buried in an unmarked grave in St. Michael's Cemetery in Bude, Cornwall, England. Her death certificate reads, "Spinster of Independent Means."

However, it's believed by some historians and occultists that Pamela Colman Smith was not quite a spinster (at least not by today's standards). While it's true that Pamela never married and was never in a long-term relationship with any man, it appeared that Pamela preferred other women's company. She spent most of her time in groups of friends within the theatre and suffragist

Pamela Colman Smith at Anne Hathaway's Cottage in 1902. Also pictured: actress Ellen Terry, Ellen's friend Lindsay Jardine, and Christabel Marshall, women's rights activist and writer.

scene, and it's believed that she may have been in a romantic relationship with a woman named Nora Lake.

Pamela and Nora had been friends for about 40 years and had been "flat-mates" for 20 of those years. After everything of value in Pamela's estate was auctioned off, everything else was willed to Nora. Some embrace the idea of Pamela's queer nature, while other researchers view her as more fluid or possibly even non-binary.

We'll never know for sure if Pamela Colman Smith was a lesbian or not. However, it could be one of the reasons why she was so quickly forgotten in the creation of the Waite-Smith tarot deck.

Pamela was eccentric and independent, which was not always celebrated in the Victorian and Edwardian Eras. She embraced her years in Jamaica and styled herself in West Indies fashion, leading many to believe that she was biracial. Pamela Colman Smith embraced what made her different (whether it was true or not), and it appears as if society shunned her for that.

With her race and sexuality in question, it's likely that she was intentionally erased from the narrative. After all, white supremacy can be found throughout the occult, including tarot.

Sadly, like the original copies of her tarot cards, Pamela Colman Smith has been lost to history. But with the help of a handful of dedicated historians and passionate tarot readers, her name (and her contribution) is being restored to its rightful place. The next time you pull your Rider-Waite-Smith tarot deck from the shelf, consider renaming it in your mind as what it truly is:

The Waite-Smith deck—celebrating the two occultists that created it: one man and one woman; one used words and the other used paint (unlocked by the power of music).

As we conclude our fourth volume of *The Feminine Macabre*, let's celebrate Pamela's quirky ways, her passion for sharing her gifts, and her courage to be herself... and may we find these traits in ourselves as well.

References:

Jensen, Frank K. *The Early Waite–Smith Tarot Editions,* p. 31.

Jensen, Frank K. (2006) *The Story of the Waite–Smith Tarot*, Croydon Hills, Australia

Kaplan, S.R. (2009). *The Artwork & Times of Pamela Colman Smith.* Stamford, Connecticut: U.S. Game Systems. p. 5.

Kaplan, S.R. (2018). *Pamela Colman Smith: The Untold Story.* Stamford, Connecticut: U.S. Game Systems. p. 11.

Palumbo, J. C. (2022, May 12). *The woman behind the world's most famous tarot deck was nearly lost in history.* CNN. https://edition.cnn.com/style/article/pamela-colman-smith-tarot-art-whitney/index.html

Place, Robert M. (2005) *The Tarot: History, Symbolism, and Divination,* Tarcher/Penguin, New York, 2005, pages 177-186

Pyne, Kathleen (2007). *Modernism and the feminine voice: O'Keeffe and the women of the Stieglitz circle.* Berkeley: University of California Press. pp. 59

Ramgopal, L. (2018, July 6). *Demystifying Pamela Colman Smith.* Shondaland. https://www.shondaland.com/inspire/books/a21940524/demystifying-pamela-colman-smith/

Ray, S. (2019, March 25). *Reviving a Forgotten Artist of the Occult.* Hyperallergic. https://hyperallergic.com/490918/pamela-colman-smith-pratt-institute-libraries/

Tea, M. (2018, September 1). The Divine Mystery of Pamela Colman Smith. *Enchanted Living Magazine.* https://enchantedlivingmagazine.com/divine-mystery-pamela-colman-smith/

Waite, Arthur Edward. *Shadow of Life and Thought.* Kessinger Publishing, page 184

MEET THE AUTHORS

LEANNA RENEE HIEBER

Leanna Renee Hieber is an actress, playwright, ghost tour guide, and the award-winning, bestselling author of Gothic, historical paranormal novels such as the *Strangely Beautiful, Magic Most Foul, Eterna Files,* and *The Spectral City* series. *A Haunted History of Invisible Women: True Stories of America's Ghosts*, Leanna's non-fiction debut, co-authored with Andrea Janes, an examination of women's narratives in haunted house and ghost stories, releases in 2022 with Kensington Books. A four-time Prism award winner and Daphne du Maurier award finalist, Leanna's books have been selected for national book club editions and translated into many languages. Her short stories have been included in numerous notable anthologies, such as *Queen Victoria's Book of Spells* and the *Castle of Horror* anthology series. *By The Light of Tiffany: A Meeting with Clara Driscoll* is a one-woman theatrical lecture Leanna adapted from the talented but little-known designer's letters and historic text. She is a licensed NYC tour guide, giving ghost tours with Manhattan's Boroughs of the Dead. Hieber has been featured in film and television on shows like *Mysteries at the Museum* and *Beyond the Unknown*, discussing Victorian Spiritualism and ghostly fascination. www.leannareneehieber.com

AOIFE SUTTON

Having completed a BA in Archaeology at University College Dublin and an MSc in Bioarchaeology at University of York, Aoife is now undertaking her Ph.D. research in the School of Archaeological and Forensic Sciences at the University of Bradford. Her research examines the anatomical collections dating to the 18th and 19th Centuries in British Institutions and what they can tell us about death and dying. She runs her own blog called the Pathological Bodies Project Blog, where she writes about a range of topics surrounding death, including archaeology, bereavement, the history of medicine, disease, and post-mortem integrity. She also works as an assistant on two death-related projects at the University of Bradford: The Continuing Bonds Project and The Dying to Talk Project. Both look at opening up conversations on death, dying, and bereavement through the use of archaeological material. She also volunteers with an embalmer and at the digital autopsy suite at her local mortuary.

AMELIA COTTER

Amelia Cotter is an author, poet, and storyteller with a special interest in the supernatural, history, and folklore. Her books include *Where the Party Never Ended: Ghosts of the Old Baraboo Inn*, *This House: The True Story of a Girl and a Ghost*, *Maryland Ghosts: Paranormal Encounters in the Free State*, the children's book *Breakfast with Bigfoot*, and the poetry collection *apparitions*. Amelia has appeared on various radio and television programs, including Travel Channel's *Hometown Horror*, and in the documentaries *Scary Stories* and *Tinker's Shadow: The Hidden History of Tinker Swiss Cottage*. She also appeared as a regular cast member on Really Channel's *The R.I.P. Files*, a paranormal reality show featuring a cast of primarily women investigators.

Visit her official website at www.ameliacotter.com or write to her any time at ameliamcotter@gmail.com

GINA ARMSTRONG AND VICTORIA VANCEK

Gina Armstrong and Victoria Vancek are the award-winning sister team, Haunted History BC. Most recently, they are recipients of the 2022 BC Heritage Award in storytelling. Their project *BC Legends and Folklore—History, Heritage, and Hauntings* was awarded recognition in the Education, Communication, and Awareness category. They are published authors, historians, and artists residing in British Columbia, Canada. Their research and writings take them to fascinating locations across the country as they delve into history, local legends, and paranormal activity. Their essays have been featured in *The Feminine Macabre* and *The Morbid Curious*. This year the sisters launched the very first Canadian paranormal magazine! *Evenings and Avenues— Hauntings in the Outskirts* was released in June 2022. Gina and Victoria continue to share their exciting adventures on several different platforms as well as on their website and social media.

You can find them on www.hauntedhistorybc.com.
Instagram @haunted_history_bc
Twitter @HauntedHistory2

RENEE BEDARD

Renee Bedard is a witch, priestess, psychic, teacher, mentor, and healing facilitator. For over a decade, Renee has offered readings, healing sessions, and mentorship that incorporate various techniques. From psychic messages, channeling, and mediumship to past life regression and Reiki, each session is unique and will focus on the client's needs at that time. Renee also holds classes, rituals, meditations, and Goddess Circles woven with myths to explore the Mysteries within us. By working with these tools, Renee feels that we can understand ourselves on a deeper level. As a result, we can begin to write our own story and understand who we are at our core.

As a student of the magical arts, Renee is currently in the Temple of Witchcraft's Mystery School, where she has recently completed her third degree with hopes to move into the fourth. She is also a Usui Reiki Master Teacher. Renee has a passion for writing about witchcraft and how she perceives the world around her. You can find her blog and nature photography on her website, thewhisperingcrow.com

REBECCA GIBSON

Rebecca Gibson is an adjunct lecturer at Virginia Commonwealth University. Her published works include *Desire in the Age of Robots and AI: An Investigation in Science Fiction and Fact* (Palgrave Macmillan 2019), *The Corseted Skeleton: A Bioarchaeology of Binding* (Palgrave Macmillan 2020), and *Gender, Supernatural Beings, and the Liminality of Death: Monstrous Males/Fatal Females* (Lexington Books 2021). She holds a Ph.D. in Anthropology from American University and, when not writing or teaching, can be found reading mystery novels amidst a pile of stuffed animals.

SARAH BLAKE

Sarah Blake resides in New Jersey but spends as much time as possible in her ancestor's home of Salem, Massachusetts. When she is not working in cemeteries and museums, she spends her time writing about forgotten history for her website HushedUpHistory.com, painting nightmares, studying mediumship and tarot, and researching all things paranormal. She has six cats and is not even <u>remotely</u> embarrassed by that fact.

STACEY RYALL

Stacey Ryall is a writer and artist from Melbourne, Australia. She holds a degree in Creative Arts from Deakin University, and her stories and articles have been published in over 20 Australian literary publications. You can connect with Stacey and her idiosyncratic projects at: https://linktr.ee/SRyall

Jillian Walkowiak

Jillian Walkowiak is a College Writing adjunct and small business owner who has spent most of her life just outside of the city of Buffalo. She has long been fascinated by history, horror, and the macabre and loves to journey down rabbit holes where she can immerse herself in any of those topics. Previous writing has included horror film and book reviews, but as time is rarely on her side, she is often relegated to grading students' writing instead of crafting her own.

TIFFINY ROSE ALLEN

Tiffiny Rose Allen is a writer and poet. Originally from the state of Florida, she started writing at an early age and self-published her first collection of poetry, *Leave the Dreaming to the Flowers,* at the age of 18. Her poetry is eclectic in portraying her views of the different aspects of life. When she is not somewhere writing, she is either creating something with her hands or working on anything and everything that excites her. Her work has been featured in numerous magazines and anthology publications, including *The Elpis Pages, Harness Magazine,* and *Dreamer by Night Magazine.* Her poetry and short story collections can be found on Amazon.

Instagram: @dreamsinhiding.writing

AMY L. BENNETT

Amy L. Bennett is a paranormal investigator and one-half of Full Dark Paranormal Explorers with her partner Ryan Bradway, based in Albany, NY. She's a multimedia artist and sometimes-blogger, obsessed with potentially haunted old houses, and hopes to one day astrally project herself successfully to the moon. Find out if it worked at fulldarkpros.com

KATE CHERRELL

Kate Cherrell is a writer, lecturer, and Ph.D. graduate, specializing in 19th Century Spiritualism in the gothic. She is the creator and editor of www.burialsandbeyond.com, a website that seeks to make death, social, and paranormal history accessible to a wider audience. She is an internationally published writer with several upcoming television appearances scheduled for 2022. She maintains an interest in paranormal investigation, cemeteries, Victoriana, and good wine.

JENNY PUGH

They say, "The dead don't speak..." but they DO to JENNY PUGH!

Naturally psychic since childhood, Jenny has encountered countless spirit visitors and ethereal entities since that time. As a talented clairvoyant medium, she can communicate with those who have passed over to the spirit world by lifting the veil that separates us. Jenny is also a paranormal researcher, writer, and psychic artist, able to produce portraits of her spirit contacts. With over 40 years of experience helping prove that our loved ones survive the thing we call "death," this medium has exhibited her clairvoyant abilities on stage, demonstrated for Spiritualist churches, and has been featured in the press. Jenny also writes articles for magazines, helping us enter a magical realm much closer than you ever imagined. Jenny's book, *Why Do Angels Have Wings?* (available on Amazon), is a poignant, funny, insightful, and captivating tale of her lifetime of supernatural experiences and is nothing short of spellbinding. From contacting the spirits of Hollywood stars to "ghostbusting" haunted houses, her intriguing memoir allows us to step into her shoes and share in her amazing adventures. You can contact Jenny at www.jennypughpsychic.com or @Jenpughpsychic on social media.

ARIANA ROSE

Ariana Rose is a student of the world, the macabre, the theatre, and North Tonawanda Middle School, where she writes for the school newspaper. Though young, she has always had a passion for writing and all things spooky. She has read most of Amanda R. Woomer's publications, and what she read has resonated with her. She is inspired by the talented women of *The Feminine Macabre* and excited to read future installments of this fascinating and important work of women in the paranormal.

ALYSSA VANG AND
TAMORA L. VANG

Alyssa has been a paranormal investigator for 16 years, along with her friends and family—including her co-author and most dearest mom, Tamora Vang. She is a big lover of cats, music, and reading all things spooky. Alyssa has worked in customer service for the past 10 years and has a creative writing BA degree. You can follow Alyssa on Instagram @alymarie90

By day Tamora works in Human Resources for a Fortune 500 company. In her off-hours, her passions include herding black cats, sewing crossbody bags that she sells in various shops, reading thrillers and cozy mysteries, exploring old buildings (both living and dead), and investigating the paranormal. Tamora owns a small paranormal team in Central New York: The AfterLife Research Agency or TARA Team.

CHELSEA CELAYA

    Currently haunting the California central valley, Chelsea Celaya considers herself a Jill-of-All-Trades with passions across the board, including sewing, themed mixology, blogging, multimedia creation through video, costumed photo shoots, and digital art, all while juggling her at-home job of mom to her toddler-aged daughter and son. She has always been interested in the macabre, fueled by her mother's love of Halloween and morbid sense of humor. When not haunting the webs of her blog, she co-hosts the podcast, *Sips & Spirits*, with her husband, where they share their love for spirits of both the alcoholic and spectral kinds by finding spooky-themed liquors and cocktails and pairing them with a creepy tale. Toast along with Chelsea by visiting her blog, cheerswithchelsea.com, or follow her on Instagram @cheers.withchelsea

STEPHANIE BINGHAM

Stephanie Bingham was born and raised in western Kentucky and could see spirits since she was a small child. She received her undergraduate degrees in history and anthropology as well as her Master's degree in history and specializes in the paranormal history of the United States. Stephanie has spent years working in museums and other haunted locations and documenting the strange occurrences there. She uses her degrees to research the paranormal and help others with talents like her own learn how to use them. Stephanie and her unique encounters have been featured as a cohost on CW's *Mysteries Decoded*, and as a guest on Destination America's *Paranormal Lockdown* and SyFy Channel's *School Spirits*. She also appears as a speaker on paranormal topics at various conventions across the country.

AMANDA R. WOOMER

Writer, anthropologist, and former international English teacher, Amanda R. Woomer (she/her) was born and raised in Buffalo, NY. She is a featured writer for the award-winning *Haunted Magazine* and *The Morbid Curious*, as well as the owner of Spook-Eats. She is the author of ten books for kids and adults, including *Harlots & Hauntings*, *A Very Frightful Victorian Christmas*, *America's Haunted Breweries, Distilleries, and Wineries*, and *A Haunted Atlas of Western New York*. She is also proud to be the creator of *The Feminine Macabre*. Follow her spooky adventures at spookeats.com and on Facebook, Instagram, and Twitter @spookeats. You can also follow *The Feminine Macabre's* journey on Facebook and Instagram @the.feminine.macabre

SARAH A. PETERSON-CAMACHO

Sarah A. Peterson-Camacho writes online for *Kings River Life Magazine*, and has been published in *MookyChick, Moonchild Magazine, Clean Sheets*, and *The Sirens Call*. She holds degrees in English and Journalism, works at a public library by day, and owns and operates Midnight Mary Antiques on Etsy. An avid ghost hunter, she has two children, 15 tattoos, and a love of all things horror, Halloween, and the paranormal.

Etsy: www.etsy.com/shop/MidnightMaryAntiques

Instagram: @midnightmaryantiques, @midnight_mary_antiques

BRIANNA BRAVOCO

Brianna Bravoco is a 29-year-old haunted history enthusiast and paranormal content creator. Brianna grew up in Doylestown, Pennsylvania, a town rich in paranormal history and lore. Brianna studied at Florida State University, where she studied Italian and is bilingual in English and Italian. Since Brianna was a little girl, she has been drawn to the curiosities of the paranormal world. Brianna has traveled to over 50 countries, searching for dark destinations and spooky encounters from beyond. Brianna focuses on urban exploration and paranormal investigations, specifically in Europe. Brianna currently lives in Berlin, Germany, and is the creator of the dark tourism Instagram "The Paranormal Passport."

SELINA MAYER AND RÉBECCA POINTEAU

Selina Mayer is an award-winning British LGBTQ+ visual artist working primarily with analog photography, specializing in nude portraiture through the "girl gaze." They studied Fine Art at Central St Martins and continue to live and work primarily in London.

Rébecca Pointeau is a funeral professional, artist, and model living in Britain. Her academic studies centered on the history of medicine, magic, art, and religion. Interest in the macabre is reflected in her art and as modeling work under the name Vulgar Superstitions.

JESSICA KRUTELL

Jessica Krutell was born and raised with an interest in the paranormal. She comes from a family of open-minded believers. Jessica is the founder of Mystic Mitten Paranormal, formed in 2017, a female-led paranormal team based out of St. Clair Shores, Michigan. With a mission of bringing light to the darkness, she hopes to make the paranormal more normal. Jessica graduated from the College of Creative Studies in Detroit with her Bachelor of Fine Arts Degree in photography. Jessica has extensive experience in the haunted house entertainment industry, making her proficient at debunking and not afraid of things that go bump in the night.

MONIQUE ROSE

Monique Rose writes and co-hosts *Fright Life: A Paranormal Podcast.* Founder of the school "Ghost Club" at 7 years old, Monique grew up interested in all things spooky. Living in an actively haunted house for most of her childhood, Monique has spent time trying to document her own paranormal experiences. Supported by the active haunted history element of her hometown of Oregon City—the end of the Oregon Trail—Monique developed a love of historical research concerning investigating the paranormal. Though the thought of capturing evidence of anomalies or proof of an afterlife is exciting, what Monique loves most is sharing stories with experiencers, enthusiasts, and skeptics alike. Telling ghost stories is ingrained in the very fabric of our humanity. Nearly every culture has its own way of sharing these tales, which connects us all. Additionally, Monique is a wife, mother, *Star Wars* cosplayer, daily quoter of *Ghostbusters*, and a lifelong student of the world.

NICOLE LONG

Nicole Long is a paranormal investigator and researcher from Salem, Virginia. She has dedicated her life to finding the macabre since she was a child, traveling all across the country in search of the unknown. Her short stories and poetry have been featured on the *Simply Scary Podcast*, *Chilling Tales for Dark Nights*, *Creepy Catalog*, *Shadows and Snow Anthology*, and *Bloodreign Magazine*. She goes by the handle @AHauntedHistory on Instagram, where she showcases her spooky travels and photography.

KACHINE MOORE

Kachine Moore is an artist, witch, projectionist, and film curator. She is the creator of Cinematic-Grimoire, a database of occult cinema, and programmer of Match Cuts Presents, a screening series dedicated to presenting de-colonialized cinema, LGBTQI films, Marxist diatribes, video art, dance films, sex films, and activist documentaries with a rotating cast of presenters from all spectrums of the performing and plastic arts and surrounding humanities. She currently resides on Long Island.

BIANCA ASCHER

Bianca Ascher is a psychic medium with 28 years of experience. Born in 1980 and raised in Germany, she recently moved to Belgium. She is well-known for her unconventional methods when communicating with the dead and formerly acted as a spiritual healer for them. She often uses elements of Hoodoo and Necromancy to bring peace to those still wandering on this earth, seeking peace and closure. She is also an experienced anthropologist (historical and cultural), which also aids her in her work.

SUSAN A. JACOBUCCI

Susan A. Jacobucci hails from Massachusetts and is an independent researcher specializing in all things paranormal. She earned a Masters in Historical Archaeology from the University of Massachusetts, Boston; BS in Anthropology from Bridgewater State University, and a BA in Sociology from Salem State University.

VANESSA WALILKO

Vanessa Walilko is a crafter, chainmailler, and chaos magician in Chicago, IL. She is the chaos engine behind PanParacon, an online paranormal conference dedicated to inclusion and diversity. She also hosts *Personal Pans*, a podcast about belief, transformation, and experiences with the weird. You can look at her aluminum jewelry at kalibutterfly.com and see her random ramblings at witchcrafts.net. You can follow her @kalibutterfly on Twitter for all her political rants and creative projects. She is available for tarot readings, both therapeutic and magickal.

JAMIE MICHELLE WAGGONER

Jamie Michelle Waggoner is a modern-day priestess, author, and folk witch. She's equally inspired by fantastical stories and the everyday magic practiced by ordinary people. She's particularly intrigued by oracular traditions, trance arts, and liminal rites.

Jamie has studied folklore, myth, and the occult since 1999. She began her priestess path as a member of the Sisterhood of Avalon for 13 years (2005-2018). She now uses her skills, empathy, and experience to lead workshops, rituals, sacred circles, and study programs. When not teaching or facilitating, Jamie writes fiction, poetry, articles, and essays and produces episodes for the *Heart of Hades* podcast. She appeared in the *Red Tent* documentary film (2012) and the *Goddess on Earth Oracle* (2021).

In addition to her independent projects, Jamie is also a co-founder and teacher for Way of the Weaver: an all-gender inclusive program of magical inquiry, social justice, and community building. You can visit Jamie online at jamiewaggoner.com and follow her @jmwaggoner on social media. *Concilio et labore, crescit eundo.*

Nikki Clement

 Nikki is a 38-year-old lifelong paranormal researcher. She resides in Louisiana with her family and cats. Her experiences with the paranormal, especially as a child, shaped her future and led her down many interesting roads in life. She is constantly researching and collecting stories, always on the hunt for hidden folklore and information. She advocates for paranormal normality in everyday life, as well as suicide and mental health awareness and education. She can be found on Facebook and Instagram as @moonmamabusiness

MARIA BLAIR

Maria Blair owns and operates No Illusions Tours in Buffalo, NY. These walking tours focus on telling the city's story from those voices not often heard, specializing in Women's History, Buffalo-based authors, and the strange and unusual tales of the city. She has lived in and around Buffalo her whole life and has studied its unique history for years. Aside from history, Maria is interested in true crime, travel, and literature.

ANN MARIE WEST

Ann Marie spent her first paycheck on a tarot deck and has never looked back. Raised in a conservative Methodist family, she is well versed in hiding in plain sight. She doesn't believe in labels. Rather if you know yourself, that is the only definition you need. Ann Marie has a BA from The University of Pittsburgh in Linguistics with a minor in Anthropology. She currently lives in Western New York with her three familiars: a Norwegian Forest Cat and two Siamese sidekicks. Her hobbies include dreamwork, tarot, and developing her mediumship abilities. Ann Marie is currently working on her first novel. A lifelong learner, you can usually find her nose in a book or trying to figure out the mysteries of the Universe. Or, perhaps, sharing whatever knowledge she has gleaned along the way with you! You can follow her on Instagram @westofwyrd

NASHOBA HOSTINA

Nashoba Hostina is a folklore enthusiast, eclectic artist, and beast of nature who, after earning their BFA, threw themself into creating works focusing on the monstrous and arcane. They live in the Midwest with their partner and two step-kitties, who all thankfully encourage Nashoba's book habit, compulsion to suddenly run off and clean up their favorite park, and tendency to eat strange plants found in the backyard.

A Special Thank you to
Lisa Morton

Photo by Seth Ryan

Lisa Morton is a screenwriter, author of non-fiction books, and prose writer whose work was described by the American Library Association's *Readers' Advisory Guide to Horror* as "consistently dark, unsettling, and frightening." She is a six-time winner of the Bram Stoker Award®, the author of four novels and over 150 short stories, and a world-class Halloween and paranormal expert. Recent books include *Calling the Spirits: A History of Séances* and *Haunted Tales: Classic Stories of Ghosts and the Supernatural* (co-edited with Leslie S. Klinger); she has been seen in such documentaries as *Demon in the White House* (Discovery +), *Shock Docs: This is Halloween* (The Travel Channel), and *The Real History of Halloween* (The History Channel).

Lisa lives in Los Angeles and online at www.lisamorton.com
Lisa on Facebook: https://www.facebook.com/lisa.morton.165
Lisa on Instagram: @lisamortoninla

BE A PART OF
THE

FEMININE
MACABRE
VOLUME V
COMING SPRING 2023

For submission guidelines, visit:
spookeats.com/femininemacabre
@the.feminine.macabre

Printed in Great Britain
by Amazon